Daphine Caruthers' Lifetime Recipe Collection

Authored by Zachary Nace

and Natalie Henley

in Loving honor of

Ella Daphine Caruthers

DEDICATION

This book is dedicated to all those who loved Daphine Caruthers.
She once said, "You will miss me when I am gone."
Never has she been so right about anything!

CONTENTS

CHAPTER 7: DESSERTS

CHAPTER 12: DRINKS 205

Introduction

The Life Story of Ella Daphine Caruthers as written in 1995.

Daphine Caruther's Parents

     A farmer man and a beautiful lady married in 1896 in a poor country place known as Lauderdale County, Alabama. He was 20 years old (born in 1876) and she was 16 (born in 1880). His father had owned lots of land on and around Blue Water cemetery and Mitchell Town. Somehow when this land was deeded, I've heard, this man (known as David Jackson Herston), was cheated out of any of it; his brother, Will Herston, got it all!

     This beautiful lady, named Ella Arty Mitchell, had a daddy known as Captain Mitchell. From this union of Jack and Ella, 14 children were born. These children were all born in the home. I, Ella

Daphine Herston, was the thirteenth child born to them on February 12, 1922.

I was born in a very small house in Anderson, Alabama. My younger sister, Katie Irene Herston, was born two years later on my birthday, February 12, 1924. She was the last child. After all, Mama was 44 when she was born.

We were poor people, but in my memory Mama and Papa were very happy. I never remember any cross words between them. My memories of living at Anderson is very vague. I do recall playing under the porch. The house was made of old planks and the porch was built high off the ground - that's the only place we could play.

My Daddy also made molasses while we lived here. I do recall going to the mill and seeing the mules going round and round. The cane was put in by hand and the mules made the "thing" turn and the juice was squeezed out. This juice was cooked down to make into molasses. My Papa raised the cane; it was hand cut and taken to the mill on a wagon. My Papa used his mill for other farmers around Anderson, Alabama.

My Papa was such a good man. He was called by everyone "Uncle Jack". He was loved by us all. My dad, at one time, owned about 200 acres in Anderson and four houses. Two at this time still stand, but are ready to fall down. I understand my sister, Georgie, and Uncle Pinky at one time lived in one of these houses and she had a child born in this house.

My dad had cancer in his upper leg, so his medical bills had to be paid. Little by little the land had to be sold. My mom inherited about $800, so we bought a home in Rogersville, Alabama. It was a big house with a big barn.

My dad was a trader - this started in Anderson before we moved to Rogersville. He had bought an old truck and would go out each morning on the back roads and buy scrap iron or anything else that he could sell and maybe make a dollar on. He tried hard to make a living to feed us children.

C.O. says he was driving the old truck to the barn one day. A big cloud came up with lots of lightning and thunder. When C.O. started to the house, a bolt of lightning hit him and he could not walk. We kids saw him and really laughed at him crawling to the house. It took him a while before he could walk. That part of the country is noted for bad storms.

I think the main reason for the move from Anderson to Rogersville was so we children could get a better education. Rogersville had a high school, so we moved to the big city of Rogersville! At least it had a school and store - I must have been about 5 or 6 years old. I did start school in Rogersville. Can't recall much about the school except - one day I was made to stand in the corner. I don't remember why I was punished. I was a good girl!

We did have to walk to school, which was about a mile away. Also, the town was about a mile so we had to walk if we went to the store. My Daddy would go to town (before he got so sick) walking. My two sisters and I would watch for him as he would always have a bag of candy for us. We'd run up the road to meet him and he'd always give the candy to Irene - she was the baby - then Mildred and I would beg.

Christmas was a happy time for us. We'd get an old cedar tree, put it in the corner of our bedroom/sitting room and we'd decorate it. We'd pop corn and string it and we'd make loops of colored paper and put that on the tree. Sure, it was pretty to us! Mama would always make an orange cake. She never used a recipe. Papa would get in the kitchen to make eggnog. He and the boys could drink it, but not us young girls. I recall one Christmas Eve my Mama stayed up to make our old dolls a dress. That's all we got except maybe an orange. Of course she was sewing by oil lamp in the same room where we slept - I was supposed to be asleep. One Christmas we really got something nice - Mama had some man to make us a biscuit board and rolling pin. They were so pretty, wish I still had them.

This room where we slept had a big fireplace in it. We had two double beds (iron stead beds). After my Papa got so sick, I was the one that had to sleep with him. I did not kick or turn too much - he got so sick. We used the big fireplace for cooking as well as to keep warm. We'd bake sweet potatoes in the hot ashes and hand a black pot and cook dried beans over the hot wood. We raised our own sweet potatoes and we'd make a hill of dirt to bury the potatoes in to keep them from freezing.

My Papa also raised or kept bees. He had several hives. He would rob the beehives and we'd have honey. My Papa had all the clothes to wear to keep from being stung.

One time we girls went down the road and dressed ourselves in poison ivy leaves. We pinned the leaves together with twigs from the bushes along the fence row. We made hats, bracelets, belts, necklaces, etc. I broke out from poison ivy so badly my eyes completely closed! I really did hurt. We did not pull that trick anymore.

A man that lived next to our home had a big apple orchard. We got run out of there more times than one.

While living at Rogersville I had double pneumonia. My parents did not think I would make it. Guess old Dr. Waddle pulled me through.

One time Mama let Irene and I go to Anderson to spend the night with my brother, Odas and his wife, Cara Lee. Irene and I went to bed (I think on the floor). My brother came home drunk. He was driving his car and was trying to come in the house with the car. I think he did get the wheels on the porch. Irene and I were so scared - she covered her head with the quilt, thought that would help! We never spent another night with them.

Sometime later Odas and family moved closer to Rogersville in a very small shack. Cara Lee had another baby - they had seven children in all. When the baby came, Cara Lee needed help to care for her and the baby. Guess who had to go? Me I! ! I knew nothing - not even how to change a diaper. I did survive, so did the rest. We laughed about this in later years.

We rented about 20 acres of land that was about 2-3 miles from our home. We had to get up real early - Mama would fix our lunch and water and off we'd go in our wagon to work all day long. We grew corn and cotton. How my Mama did so much work I'll never know. She worked from daylight to dark all her life. I remember the hot sun and trying to find a shade tree. I was too small to do the work.

I remember a fig tree grew outside the one window of this room where we sat and slept. One time at school I got lice. I sat by that same window to comb out the lice with a fine tooth comb. We had no medicine for this kind of thing. We had no electricity nor inside toilets. We had to go outside, rain or shine, to use the toilet. We had not toilet paper, we only had Sears catalogs! My sister-in-law, Nell, had a baby at our house. They told us he had come from Sears - we looked everywhere for the box! This man now lives in Akron, Ohio (Jim Herston) . My two cousins also stayed with us for a while in Rogersville to go to school; they were Uncle Wills' (Papa's brother's girls) Kathleen and Ethel. As usual, our Mama was so good to them and good to keep them as she had about seven still at home. My brother, C.O., was Mama's best help - he'd get out on that old back porch and do the washing, in the winter time.

My Dad and the boys would kill hogs - they killed them and hung them up to drain out the blood. This took place at the old barn behind the house. The barn still stands on Rose Street in Rogersville.

Our Papa became worse every day. Our oldest brother, Robert, had a car so he'd come and take Papa to Nashville, Tennessee's St. Thomas Hospital. He'd take treatments and more strong medicine so he'd not hurt. He was taking Morphine, I'm sure. Finally he got so bad they could do no more for him in Tennessee. He was put in a hospital in Birmingham, Alabama to have his leg amputated. He had taken so much strong medicine that when they cut his leg he had nothing stronger to take. I've been old (to my sorrow) that you could hear him holler all over the hospital - isn't that sad? It makes me cry just to think about it. His cancer had spread up in his body.

My sister-in-law, Nell (Henry's wife), had a chocolate cake in the oven of the old wood stove for us to eat. We young children were getting ready to go see our Papa when we got the word that our precious Papa was dead. The cake was for us to eat on the way to the hospital. Will Burch (Aunt Missie's first husband) was gonna take care of us while Mama was gone. I was 10 years old. What a sad time for Mama - left with all us kids and no money. I can well remember one thing Mama said, "One never knows what it's like until they go through it." The funeral was at Blue Water Cemetery in Mitchell Town. The service was outside at the graveyard. All I could see sitting down was my Papa's nose. I sure recall the song "Amazing Grace". Even now when I hear that song, tears come to my eyes. This song has been sung at seven brothers and two sister's funerals. I hope it will be sung at mine.

I can't remember much that took place in Rogersville after that. Mama could not make it, so we moved below Florence on

Cloverdale Highway. Sure not better there! We lived in a big house with a big front porch. We really had a rough time. We had to heat the water to wash clothes in and carry it up a hill. We had a washboard to scrub the clothes with. Our laundryman (C.O.) had married while we lived here - I remember the time he married (C.O.). They came to stay their first night at Mama's house. One of my older sisters was there. They slipped into C.O.'s room and sewed the bottom of Ruby's gown together. They thought it funny, but I did not see anything to laugh about. See, I was a good girl!

Our home burned to the ground in Rogersville, so we had no money from that, no insurance. This happened just after we moved out, probably 6 months after we moved from Rogersville.

We planted corn mostly and we worked in the fields. Mama had a cousin there to help out, Vandy Mitchell. We kept missing grain out of our barn and came to find out Vandy was sacking it up and selling it. We were sharecropping on this big farm. Sharecropping is you raise the crops and the owner gets half the profit. Needless-to-say we went broke, thanks to Vandy. I've had no use for him after that. He's dead now, but he had a son, Horace Mitchell. Each time I see Horace I think of this. I'm sure Horace knows nothing about this.

While we lived on the farm the big tornado in Tupelo, Mississippi happened. We found things from that storm on our land. One time walking up the lane to our house I had to walk across a small branch - I saw a snake as long as a hoe handle. I screamed and someone came to kill it. Sometimes we did not have enough to eat, most every night all we had was milk and cornbread. If we had a bowl of Cornflakes, that was a real treat. Mama made all our dresses, not even a pattern. Our dresses were mostly made from feed sacks. We wore our dress to school, when we came home we had to take it off so we could wear it the next day. The only way we kept bathed was out of a wash pan, homemade lye soap and a rag. We had no toothbrushes, just a stick or rag with salt and soda on them. Now lye soap - we made at hog killing time in a big black pot outside. I really don't know how except it was out of hog grease - of course, Mama knew everything!

Not any of our yards had grass on them. We never said "the yard needed mowing." It had to be swept clean with a handmade broom, straw tied together with some wire and put on a stick. See how easy life was!

We made our playhouse in the dirt yard. We marked out rooms with sticks. We played hopscotch and marbles a lot also in the dirt yard. We all had chores to do - bring in the wood to cook with and heat the house with the fireplace. We had to sweep out the floors and help Mama cook. We always did the dishes - Mildred and I, of course - Irene was the baby and spoiled, so she did not help much. She says that's not true!

Mama used snuff (ground up tobacco). She'd sit at night and chew on a stick, put the stick in her box of snuff, work it around her mouth, then spit it in the fireplace. I really did hate this. I'd usually go out, that's the only thing I disliked about my mom. I still don't like tobacco in any form. My Papa did not use it and he hardly drank whiskey that I know about. I do remember one time he drank some whiskey and it really made him sick. He did not admit to us kids that he had drank too much. He said he swallowed a fly!

I don't remember how long we lived in this house below Florence, but it wasn't long. We moved on a road, can't think of the name, but the place was called McGee Town. We lived in a real small house with steps to the attic or bedroom. My brother, Robert, had given me a set of 6 little dolls in a box. I fell down those steps and broke them all. I cried my eyes out. I remember Robert coming to our house and he'd call Mama out so he could give her a little money, that way Aunt Tammie would not know this. He helped Mama out a lot, but I'm sure she could have used more help.

We picked cotton all day and got paid for this. We hired out to other people. Mama made our cotton sacks. They were domestic material, about 6 feet long, with a strap to go around our neck to pull the bag. We had to crawl on our knees or bend over to pick the cotton. Usually we did both sides of the rows at a time. The bag got so heavy, we had to take it to the wagon to have it weighed and emptied. We probably made $1 a day. Boy, when we got home Mama's food tasted so good. I mostly remember her puddin' and sauce made by guess on a wood stove. She was a great cook, I thought. We had a long table that we could all eat together. One side had a bench that was as long as the table, then straight chairs was used on the other side and the ends. After eating, the men would go on the front porch and lay down to rest.

After this small house we moved into a house on the other side of the road and about a mile off that road. This house still stands. We lived in this house with a Mrs. Thrasher - she was Annie Dee's (Lee's first wife) grandmother. Lee and Annie Dee married while we lived there. My first memories of this place was the 4th of July at a park where they made stew. This was the first time I ever heard of ice cream cones. They had homemade ice cream. We used to bite the bottom out of the cones and such the cream out. Also, we got different flavors and take a lick from each others.

Mildred says all I ever did was follow in her footsteps and if she did or said anything wrong I would tell on her to Mama. Of course, I always had all her old leftover clothes. Missie also gave us anything her girls did not want. They had things we never had. Also at Missie's and Will Burch's house is the first inside toilet I ever used. We all thought they were rich. That house still stands. Missie was always so good to Mama and Papa - she should have a star in her crown!

While we lived at Mrs. Thrasher's, Missie and Will moved to outside Mt. Pleasant, Tennessee. Will ran a corn mill, Missie got a job in Columbia at one of the factories. C.O. and Ruby helped at the mill. Soon Missie and Will moved to Columbia and she kept boarders. Finally she talked Mama into moving to Columbia. I visited our last home at McGee Town in 1994. It was a happy day for me, it had been about 56 years since we moved away. The house sure brought back memories of days when we slept with our doors unlocked and windows open. When we lived there a fence was across the back. We would come in hungry from school, we'd get a piece of cornbread and go out and pull up an onion, sit on that fence and eat. We thought that was so good.

We grew lots of Irish potatoes. I fussed when I had to help pick them up. Mama said to me one time, "Why do you fuss at picking up potatoes as well as you like them." I've always loved potatoes, any .way they are fixed. I liked helping Mama in the kitchen. One time I was gonna beat the egg whites by hand (no electric then). I was beating away and I dropped eggs, bowl and all. The bowl broke all to pieces. My "sweet" sister, Mildred, kept telling Mama "whip her, whip her". My Mama said to Mildred, "If you helped sometime, you might break something too!" That was that.

Sometimes on Sundays we made iced tea, what a treat! We had a big block of ice that had to be chipped. Tea sure was better back then - we had no Cokes, at least we did not. We left this home in Alabama and left some of our hard times, but not all.

Well -- here we are in the big city of Columbia, Tennessee on East 9th Street. We rented a house from Mr. Will Cranford, known as Mr. Republican! He and his wife and daughter were nice to all of us. Mama kept boarders in this house. Now Mr.

Cranford decided he needed his house to live in, so another move for us. We then moved up the street about two houses and rented from Mr. John Crowe. Mr. Crowe ran a grocery store next door to this house. I had some happy times here. School was about 8 to 10 blocks away. Of course, we all walked together. I moved in the middle of a school year. I only took 3 subjects and I failed one. I went to Columbia High School 4 1/2 years and graduated with 18 credits with an average of 86. I beat Katie Sue Pinkston (Foster) and Daisy Jones (Jeter). That made it all just fine.

My life with Katie Sue started soon after I moved to Tennessee. She and I met in the study hall. We liked each other from the start. I used to ride the bus home with her (big deal for me) and spend the night. Her mom always treated me special, she'd either cut a country ham or kill a chicken for me. We ate well. Mrs. Pinkston went to a lot of trouble for us and our dates. On Sunday night she'd fix us a table in the parlor with sandwiches or a pineapple cheese salad on it. It would be waiting for us when we came in. I was dating Wilburn Fitzgerald and Sue was dating his cousin, Allen Fitzgerald. The worst thing (almost) we did while dating them was we skipped school one day (played Hookey). We went riding, walking - laughing until time for school to be out. We had to write notes and we did get by with this. Mama and my brothers were very strict with us girls.

One time I had a date - the guy drove up and blew his horn for me to come out. My brother, I think Taylor, was visiting us. He goes out and runs the date away. He told my date never to blow for me again!

Daphine Caruthers in front of South Main Street Home

I met A.E. along this time at a skating rink somewhere in south Columbia, 14th or 15th Street. He comes up to me and asked, "Are you Daphine or Irene Hern?" I told him, then he asked to drive me home. I told him no. Later on that night he saw me in the car with someone else. It made Gene so mad, he was driving on the wrong side of the road! My Mama loved Gene so much. When I didn't like something Gene did and got mad at him Mama would tell Gene never to come back to see me again. She'd say, "You are too good to her". Gene would be waiting for me each afternoon after school to drive me home. I sat in physics class and could see his car waiting on me. Usually we'd go to Denkams for Coke or ice cream. It was a place for young people to "hang out" on South Main Street. It was a neat place to go. The first time Gene ever took me out for dinner in Franklin I was so nervous I thought I did not know the proper way to eat. This place was across from the Oldsmobile car place on Columbia Avenue in Franklin. Gene took me out to lots of places. I'm sure I'd never gone had it not been for him. We always drove to the Lawrenceburg Fair in the fall - they had a really good fair. We'd have those stupid pictures made.

One time Mama let me go with him to Leavy, Arkansas. Gene had an aunt there - Aunt Mae and Uncle Ed. We had a good time, they were nice to me. We only stayed a few days.

It seemed like I'd never get through high school. One time my male teacher caught me and Smith Dotson talking. We had to stay after school. This teacher thought we were sweethearts, he was so wrong. Smith and I were only friends. Some of us always had to stay after school in Mr. Carl Gardner's history class - I did not like history and I wasn't very good, but I did pass.

Katie Sue and I were always together all through high school. Another girl, Daisy Jones, was our friend also. Katie Sue and I always went to Mule Day - she would spend the, night at my house and we'd walk uptown and stay all day except to come home to eat. I never had any money to eat out. One year someone brought some rides, Farris Wheels, etc. They were set up behind the old bank and across from Foster Insurance now. We had more fun than anyone. Also, one time on Mule Day this band came to town. They had a dance at the tobacco barn on 8th Street and Woodland Street. The big band was The Tommy Dorsey Band - they were big. I did go, but since I could never dance, I did not stay that long. Katie and I had dresses alike also one Mule Day. We were the cutest young girls on the street.

I also played in the first band the high school ever had. I played the clarinet under the direction of Tom Hewgley. We marched in a white skirt and blouse, no uniforms. I remember the blue ribbon parade - going down West 7th Street. I just remember one trip we took to Clarksville, Tennessee. Sure, I could play. One afternoon I was leaving school, on foot, and Tom Hewgley asked if I cared for a ride downtown. Of course I did. He parked in front of the old Waldridge Drug Store. He looked in his mirror and said, "I'd better comb my hair or someone will say we've been out on the Theta Pike." I just thought that was awful, a teacher saying that to little ol' me.

Daphine Caruthers enjoying Mule Day in Columbia, TN

Mildred and Irene were both married before I graduated. I was the only one to finish high school out of Mama's 14 children. My family did real well, had good jobs and nice homes and cars - once we got out of Alabama. I've said many times while driving our Olds down those same roads in Alabama that I rode in an old wagon that I'd never dreamed of ever having a car to ride in - I'm so thankful.

During my high school days I had several boyfriends, besides

Gene, on the string. None I liked, but they had cars and I almost always double dated with Daisy or Katie Sue. I got several nice gifts from some, like a gold locket and a cedar chest. One of my children has the chest now. The one that gave me the chest told me "I'd better not ever see Gene Caruthers clothes in it". Of course, he never did, as I didn't like that guy anyway.

There was no way I could stay out late and my Mama not know when I came in. You see, I slept with her. The bed we slept on was a four-poster bed in Aunt Georga's house now. We had all the rooms rented out to working men. We had at least a dozen lunches to fix each day. We also got up and cooked a big breakfast, we girls had to help. The meal at supper time was a big meal. Mama was always noted for her good food. Would you believe some people left and never paid her for staying there? How could anyone do a widow woman that way?

We left 9th Street and moved to a larger house on North Garden, now the Nashville Highway. Our house stood about where Sherwin Williams was for years. I didn't know how long we lived there, but we sure kept a lot of men. The house was real large. We had as many as three beds in the upstairs rooms, which meant we had the beds to make up and change sheets every week. Such an easy life! We sure did not complain to Mama.

Our next move was to North Main Street. This was a small house and just above the river bridge. We lived here when Irene and Toby married, January 1941. Our little Tommy Potts was also a baby when we lived here, we all adored that child. He was so beautiful to be a boy baby. We kept him a lot for Mildred. We spoiled him rotten. Guess that's what caused him to go bad - he's been in prison most of his adult life.

I graduated from high school while we lived on North Main Street. I remember my graduation day very much. The auditorium was really full. Gene came and he said he got up to give someone his seat and he left. He could not stand long enough to see me get my diploma! I was already mad when I noticed he was gone. We got home in time for me to see Gene's car coming across that bridge with a girl in there with him. Of course, he carried her right home, then back to me. I told him I never wanted to see him again and I really did mean that. It took months for him to get back in my good graces. Even now it makes me mad!!

June, 1941 - One thing that took place at my graduation I'm ashamed to tell. I'd have had a fit had my children pulled this stunt! Who's idea it was I don't remember, now that's not important! Daisy, Katie Sue and I decided we'd get on the Mt. Pleasant Pike and hitchhike to Mt. Pleasant - this we did. This salesman came by and stopped so we all piled into his car. I think we all sat in the front seat. Of course, the man had to shift the gears and guess who was sitting close to him. He made several stops at grocery stores. We realized later on how stupid that was for us to do. We laugh about it now, but it could have turned out so differently.

Well, again we moved, this time to South Main Street. Gene goes in Service October 1941, while we lived in this house. Gene sent me money to come to Norfolk, Virginia on the bus. Mama would let me go anywhere to him or with him. Gene asked me to marry him, so we did on November 29, 1941. We stayed with a Mrs. Jaymes in Norfolk. I did not stay long as Gene was shipped out. Then it was back home to Mama.

From the small house on South Main we moved to Clarksville, Tennessee, 744 Franklin Street. Mama took our Susie with us. Susie was a black cook that had helped Mama for some time.

Missie and her family lived in Clarksville, so that's why Mama moved there. Susie had her own room off the back porch. She also was a wonderful cook. We all loved her. She was honest and faithful. The last years of her life she worked for Mr. and Mrs. Bob Alderson. Mama did not need her then as we did not keep as many boarders. She died while working for the Aldersons. I'd always ask about Susie when I'd see Marcie or Bob Alderson.

While living in Clarksville, Jessie Palmer boarded with us. She and I were on the big front porch one day. Hoyt came home on leave from Service. She and Hoyt started dating and they were married.

Gene's ship docked at Mere Island, California - of course, he sent for me. I took the train across country to San Francisco where Gene met me. I think Mrs. Caruthers went with me the first time I went to California. She did not stay long, but I stayed on. That train ride was so great, I loved it - eating in the diner and sleeping in a berth. This country girl from Alabama was a "fir piece away". Gene and I got a room in Vallejo, California. I stayed there while his ship went out, maybe for months. I had to ride a ferry over to work. Of course I walked to the ferry. I worked in blueprints. We, rather they, repaired ships on this island. I had that Alabama drawl, so people would come talk to me, just to hear me talk. This is the first time I had eaten and worked with blacks. Coming from Alabama, this was very strange. I really could not get used to this, now some of my best friends are black. I think we lived this way almost a year.

We left California as Gene was to go to Miami, Florida for training. We visited Mama in Harriman, Tennessee, as she had moved once again. Can't remember much about this town except a college was on a street behind where Mama lived. We left and went to Nashville Depot and rode the Flagler to Florida. We stayed in a room on Flagler Street. I used to watch as Gene marched along that street. We had a small apartment, but one evening we went to a restaurant to eat. We ordered - the green pea soup came first. I ate a few bites and up it all came, right in my soup bowl. We got up and left. I had to stop along the street to do it again. Yes, I was pregnant - Janice Faye. Gene would get up and fix me bacon and eggs and then he'd go to work. As soon as he left I'd get rid of that stinking stuff - I was so sick. So Gene took me home to Mama. Now Mama lived on South Main and 13th Street. This was a big house with a porch on two sides. She lived here a long time.

Sometime during my pregnancy, early part I think, I rode the train back to San Francisco, California to the christening of the Eislie. I was invited to do this. I have a picture of me on the top deck of this ship at the ceremony. Of course, Gene was shipped out again and back to Mama I went.

It was this house that I came home to with my little girl that was born at King's Daughters Hospital. I named her Janice Faye. It's not the name Gene and I had decided on, but I thought the name was right after I saw her. He saw her for the first time about one year later. We had named her Patricia Jean. She only knew the picture of Daddy by our bed. Mama and Irene really helped out with her - she was the joy of all our lives. We did not see much of the other grandmother - she refused to come see us. I'd take Janice once in a while to see her. She really did not pay much attention to her. That was her loss.

Sometimes I'd get mail at Mrs. Caruther's house. She would take it to Aunt Francis to bring to me. Francis lived between me and Mrs. Caruthers. The whole trip to my house was all of two blocks!

Janice was one year old when her Daddy came home. For the first time he saw his little girl. He had several days leave and we packed up and went to Orange, New Jersey. We had a two room apartment. The houses were built next to one another and right on the sidewalk. No yards at all. We did not have a car, so we had to ride the subway. We spend Easter of 1945 in New Jersey. I had Janice dressed so cute, bonnet and all. I have pictures of her.

We had fun at this town, so close to New York City. We took in Barnum & Bailey Circus at Madison Square Garden. We also went to see the Rockettes at the theatre in Rockefeller Center. We had a babysitter for Janice Faye that night. We rode the subway one day and went to the Statue of Liberty. We walked to the top of her. We also walked on Caney Island.

We decided to go shopping one day while living in New Jersey, so we go by subway to New York. We walked in I.J. Fox fur store for me, a fur coat. We did not see one coat. This lady came to wait on us and told me to take a seat. She asked me what I had in mind and how much I wanted to spend. Then they brought out several coats for me to choose from. The coat hangs in my closet now. We went in Lord and Taylor and I bought a new dress for Easter. I thought I had a special dress and no one at home would have one like it. First one I saw at home had on a dress just like mine.

We were walking in our neighborhood one night and I saw this green duck. I just had to have him. The next day when the store opened I was there to buy my duck. He is in the china cabinet now. We also went to the Empire State Building. It was over 100 stories tall. We looked down and cars looked like ants.

We went to another ship christening. This ship was the Rolette. Gene had to go out on the ship from the Atlantic through the Panama Canal, to San Francisco on to Hawaii, then to the Philippines. All his ships carried ammunition. Peace was declared and Gene came home.

Gene got out of the Navy and got a job in Alabama working out of the local in Sheffield. We boarded at Mrs. Starkey's in Florence, that was neat. Food ready for us three times a day, Janice was the belle of the ball. She was learning to walk and I dressed her adorable. I could not stand for her to ever get dirty. Everyone there thought she was so good and adorable, we did too. Again I got pregnant. We lost the fetus and Aunt Missie lived there in Florence and she saw to me. She has always been so good.

One time Janice and I were in Columbia at Mama's, but we needed to go back to Daddy in Florence. C.O. said that he'd take us, it was snowing some, but before we got to the state line the roads were slick and cars were all over the roads. After about 3 hours we made it, I was scared to death. I was afraid we'd all freeze.

Well, Gene's job finished in Alabama, so here we go again -- we took off for Detroit, Michigan. Gene went to see a friend he knew in the Service - they were nice to us. It just so happened his parents had died and their house was vacant - had all the furniture in it, so we just moved in. It was a lovely two-story home. While Gene, Janice and I lived there Charles, (Gene's brother), came to visit us. He stayed in this home with us until we left. I got pregnant again and I was really sick. I just wanted my Mama and to go home to Columbia. Well, my Mama and Irene came to Detroit. Gene decided to quit his job and drive us all back to Tennessee. Charles stayed, he got a job and later on married Margie, where he still lives. Mrs. Caruthers always blamed us for Charles leaving home! This is when we bought the first home we ever owned at 700 Riverside Drive. My one and only boy was born while we lived here. Don Richardson built our home and he lived next door to us. He said Mike was the prettiest baby he ever saw. Granny Russel lived on the other side of our home. She kept Mike some for me, he played with cans and pulled the labels off. He also like to play in dried beans and peas.

Brother Fred Blankenship used to pick up Janice for church. Everyone talked about how cute she was. I know she was a good girl. I also joined Riverside Methodist Church in 1947. I was baptized in the Duck River - at a Mr. Grey's camp.

My sister, Mildred, had a little girl while we lived in this home. She would not name her, so I named her Donna Jean. I also took care of Mildred and baby until they could go home. Gene and Billy Parchment built a picket fence around the front yard. Sure made our place look better. We loved that house! When we moved into this

31

home we had not cook stove and could not buy one. You had to sign up and wait your turn. Mr. Jack Carlton came out to our house and saw me, big as a cow. Thanks to Mike, he said, "You sure need a stove to cook on." I was using a hot plate.

That same day he had me a stove delivered. I always loved Mr. Carlton after that and bought all my other appliances from him. We were happy here until Gene came home one day and said he had taken a job in Baton Rouge, Louisiana. Gene and Roy had a service station on South Main Street that could not make us all a living, so Gene sold his part to Roy. We sold our lovely home for $9,000, the same price we had paid for it. Mr. N.J. Adams bought it. He is the man that took Granddaddy Mike's job on the railroad.-

In Baton Rouge we rented a duplex - nice enough. It has swings out back for the children to play on. We settled in down there, joined a church. Janice was an angel in their Christmas play. I drank strong coffee there and ate lots of good spaghetti. People there sure know how to make it. I tried to learn how, but never like those Louisiana people. Meatball and spaghetti was really good. C.O. got a job also in Baton Rouge. We enjoyed having him living in this same town. We lived on Plank Road and when it rained we could not get in our house unless we took off our shoes. The land was so low.

We enjoyed living in Baton Rouge, but here we moved again. This time was the worst. We lived with Mrs. Caruthers. I felt very unwanted. Of course, Gene went to work each day and I stayed home with Janice and Mike. Mrs. Caruthers made it clear we were a hardship on her and I'm sure we were. She told me, "You'll have to get out and find a place to live. As long as Gene has food on the table and a place to sleep, he'll never look further." Well, that I did. I found a house to rent on Dimple Court. It belonged to T.H. Cook. It was very comfortable, but small, two bedrooms. We knew Wayne Potts and his family that lived across the street. They went to our church - R.U.M. Church. We took turns cooking for each other every week.

Soon T.H. Cook needed his house, so we moved again to 1817 Parkway Drive. I was pregnant again when we moved into this house. Edna Marie was born during the time we had the worse ice/snow storm on record, January 28, 1951. Just as she and I left the King's Daughters Hospital the electricity went out. Then as the ambulance drivers carried me in our back door our electricity went out. We thought we'd all freeze to death. Mama was there, bless her, to help me out. Pat Garrell lived next door to us, she took over the job of bathing Edna Marie. Gene got Bob Hunter to open his store (it was either after hours or on Sunday) and we bought a small oil heater. It kept mine and the baby's room warm, thanks be to God!

Francis Caruthers had kept Mike and Janice. Mike cried for his Mama and his Mama cried for him. Janice was a big girl, but Mike was a Mama's boy and I loved that! Francis had to cook in her fireplace, like my youth days! We made it through that ordeal, I don't know how.

Well would you believe we made another move? This time we moved to 5th Avenue in a house that belonged to Mr. and Mrs. Steenburger. We had the downstairs and the upstairs was rented to someone else. It was also a small place, Gene and I slept in the living room. The next door neighbors were the Connelly's. We had known them for some time. They had several dogs and when the kids went outside to play, those dogs would act like they would eat them up. The dogs tried to get over the fence at them, I think that is why Edna Marie is so scared of dogs to this day! It was a good place to live otherwise. Kids could ride bikes to school and we were close to church.

But with our family, all good things must come to an end. We moved again — this time we bought a duplex in Greenwood Acres. We lived on one side and Norman and Colleen Fraser lived in the other. We loved that couple very much and their daughter, Brenda. They lived with us for several years. When Brenda got school-age they had to move to Nashville to put her in school for the hard of hearing, the Bill Wilkerson School. Norman got a job with one of the T.V. stations and later he worked for W.S.M.V. as cameraman. Colleen was one of the most beautiful young ladies I ever met. She was beautiful inside as well as out. She died several years later in Nashville from heart problems. I still miss her.

Next door, Mr. and Mrs. Hubert Fraser lived - they were jewels also. Across the street lived Mr. and Mrs. James Haywood and Gayle; also across lived Mr. and Mrs. Aubry Nelson, Bonnie and Debbie. On the other side of my home lived Sarah and Charles Fraser and Linda Gayle. Now this is the same Sarah White I know now. Her life is another story, but we became very close friends through many hard times. One time she wanted to learn to sew, so here she comes down for me to help her. She may be smart, but I assure you - sewing was not her talent. I told her then I'd never try to help anyone else learn to make anything!

She got pregnant and it was time for the baby. She was ready and wanted to get it over with. I told her to take some Castor oil, believe me, she thought she was gonna die. Anyway, she gave birth to Charles Henry (Chuck). We did a lot together when we had money, like shopping. One time she got her billfold swiped in Nashville, I think she had $20, which is like $2,000 now.

We lived in Greenwood Acres several years. The children rode the bus to Riverside School. Mike had a good friend that lived close by, David Brown, and they lived just down the street. We really outgrew this 2 bedroom/1 bath house, so we sold out. We built a house in Hardy Acres. We had three bedrooms, den and two bathrooms. We had a full basement. Also, two acres of land. We had a garden, fruit trees and walnut trees. Gene and Mike decided we needed a swimming pool. With fork and shovel and Mike Law, they started digging. They did a lot, but finally they needed help, so Redbird came over and got the hole dug. We had a really nice pool and the children did enjoy it. Daddy was the one that had to take care of it.

One Christmas I could not find Mike, I called everywhere. No one had seen him. I was about to call the law when Gene said maybe he went back to Greenwood Acres. I called the lady we had sold to and he had been there. He and Mike Law had walked there, ax in their hands to cut down a cedar tree we had planted in the back yard of our former home. The lady would not let him cut it down. Mike could not understand since we had planted it, why he couldn't have it.

Janice met Carroll while we lived here - yes, she also married him. I thought my world had come to an end when she left. I could not eat, I did not even want to cook. I could not understand her wanting to marry. She had a pretty room in our basement (this is what she wanted), we kept her in pretty clothes and we had her ready to go to college. She gave it all up -- soon we had our little Kimberly, our first grandchild. She was so precious. I went to work at Sears. Katie Sue called and begged me to work with her, so I did. Two years later Karen

Daphne was born to Janice - now we had two little girls.

Edna Marie was still in Riverside School. She and Mike rode the school bus, I had to carry her to the bus stop as she was so afraid of dogs. I was room mother chairman at Riverside School, I really worked hard on that deal. I was also Cub Scout leader for Mike - I made their crafts while they played. What a thankless job. Mike was so much trouble, he'd want something then when he got it he was through with it. Like the tent he had to have. One night in it, he didn't want it anymore. We got him a T.V. set one Christmas. He was not one bit happy. "It's the worst Christmas I ever had." Of course we had to cut down on the girl's gifts since the T.V. cost so much. Gene and I thought he'd be so happy. Our three children have always loved Christmas at home. I'm glad - Gene worked long, hard hours - snow, rain and sleet to make us have nice things and we did.

One day our friend Sarah asked Gene to sell our home in Hardy Acres. Sarah was trying her hand in real estate, working for John Early. She told Gene what she thought it was worth, but Gene told her what he'd take. She said it would never bring that, but the right one came by and bought our pretty home.

Now another move - we rented a nice home in Pleasant Hills. All the time we lived there we were looking for another home to buy. I was riding around one day and saw this sign in the yard for sale on Sunnyside Drive. I took the number and we called for an appointment. By the way, we had already bought this lot at 4014 Trotwood. Gene and I looked at the house in Sunnyside and he really did like it. They told us what they were asking and Gene made an offer. They really wanted to sell, so we had bought us a house. I hated Sunnyside — bunch of snobs — Gene asked me to try living there for one year and if I still didn't like it, he's build me a house on our lot. Of course, after he said that I really didn't try to like it! Again, Sarah sold this house and again made a good profit for us. Sarah had a house for rent in Barrow Court. We should have bought this home - $16,000 and it had a rental apartment upstairs.

One day there - I was resting on the couch - when in came Edna Marie and this young man. She went through, then here he came - "Hi, *I'm* Emmitt Webb". Then on to the kitchen. He hasn't changed one bit, he always hits the kitchen first.

**Daphine Caruthers with husband, Gene
at Trotwood Home**

Rex Pogue finally got our house done at 4014 Trotwood. Of course, Gene came out every night and put more nails in. We moved in on a rainy muddy day. We had our house paid for, but we were completely broke. I worked for the censors, then along came G.E. I was lucky enough to get a job, that was in 1971. We finally got on our feet, but we worked hard. The yard was a muddy mess, but Gene worked hard on it. Soon people were telling him he sure had a pretty yard. This house is not a mansion, but it's been home longer than any I've ever had. I like it here - I'm sorry if you don't.

Edna Marie got married to Mitch while we lived here. Now she has three daughters, Natalie Renee, Stephanie Marie and Ashley Elizabeth.

Michael married Claudia Gillespie and they have a boy and girl, Mike Jr. and Sally Douglas. Janice had two boys besides Kimberly and Karen her girls. The boys are Christopher Eugene and Ernest Kevin. As of 1994 we have three great grandsons. If we live long enough, I'm sure we'll have more greats as we have nine grandchildren. What a life!

During Janice's school days she was a joy. Sure, she had wants, but if she asked one time and we said no, that would be the end of it. She never kept on begging. She went through several years of being a Girl Scout. Mrs. Dalton White was her leader. The same girls stayed together all those years.

Janice's best friend was Linda Gayle Parks. They had camping trips, overnight sleep-outs at the Monsanto Camp. I helped Mrs. White some, she and I had a float in the Mule Day Parade, doing most of the work ourselves. She was a wonderful leader. Janice did well in school, but she had to study hard. I'm sure she doesn't remember all the nights I stayed up sewing for her. I made all her clothes, even her coats. Also I made some adorable doll clothes for her dolls at Christmas time. I had made her an adorable taffeta dress. She had worn it to a party and fell down and tore that pretty dress. She was afraid to come home and show me. I can't remember being too mad; I knew she did not mean to - somehow I repaired the dress.

When Janice learned how to drive it was a big help to me. I ran a taxi all the time - church, work, and school work for my family. She also was a good helper in the kitchen. You can see why I wanted to keep her home.

Now Mike was another story. He was always a troublemaker at home. His teachers said he was so good at school and church. After all, he seemed to be the "teacher's pet"! Mike could have been real smart had he tried. He'd read something and say he knew all about it - he never really studied. He made pretty good grades. Mike began playing ball as soon as he could hold a ball and bat. His Daddy saw to that! I had to take Mike for a haircut, but his Dad took him to ball practice - of course, I did too. Ball really kept us all busy. It was either practice or a game all the time. Hot dogs were our main menu.

Christmas time with Daphine Caruthers

Poor baby, Edna Marie hated every minute of this. She did not like to go, but she had no choice. Gene never coached Mike, but believe me, he coached from the stands. Gene would tell Mike all the things he did wrong after every game! Then when Mike did really good, "That's My Boy!" Mike played basketball throughout high school. He was very good. He was co-captain with Tommy Yokley in his senior year. Mike went on to Tennessee Tech in Cookeville, Tennessee. He and Claudia were married in the Chapel of Riverside United Methodist Church. Mike is now a Lieutenant Colonel in the U.S. Army. He might have done better had he joined the Navy!!

Edna Marie was named after two of my sisters - her Daddy named her. Edna did well in school. She like to sing and took voice lessons from Mrs. Faye Robinson. She sang at her graduation, she did real good. She also sang in the choir at church and she sang solos also there. Edna went to Columbia State for a year, then she went to Tennessee Tech. She had met Mitch Webb at Columbia State, so he also transferred to Tennessee Tech. After they finished college they were married. They now have three daughters, Natalie, Stephanie and Ashley!

Gene stayed in the Naval Reserve for 39 years after coming home from the war years. He went to meetings at the old Institute where the Post Office, Fred's, etc. now stand. That beautiful building burned. You could see the fire for miles. Gene went to Shelby Park to meetings sometimes. Janice, Mike and Edna Marie and I would go with him. It was always a treat to drive up to Nashville. He also had to go to Charleston, South Carolina to the U.S. Naval base for two weeks of school. Our whole family went along - we rented a trailer and lived in it for two weeks. You kids wanted to stay. That was August 1955. We lived in Greenwood Acres at that time. We drove around and saw the old city of Charleston. We saw the ocean and the beach was very dirty from a storm. Our trailer was next door to the railroad tracks. When the trains came by it seemed like they were coming through our bedrooms. The trailer would shake and rock. Gene made a grade of 3.5 and we have his certificate to prove it!

Daphine Caruthers

Chapter 1: Salads

Cabbage Salad by Geneva

Grate cabbage to suite you Usually 1 good apple is enough 4-5
stems of celery, raisins I have no amount of this I use a spoon of
mayonnaise, some cool whip, 1 teaspoon vinegar, 1 teaspoon sugar.
The vinegar or lemon juice will keep fruit better. Better made the day
of use.

Here's what's cooking: Cabbage Salad
Recipe from the kitchen of: Geneva's

Grate Cabbage to suit you. Usually
1 good apple is enough. 4 - 5
stems of Celery, Raisins —
I haad' no amount of this —
I use a spoon of mayonnaise
some Cool whip 1 tsp vinegar
1- tsp sugar. the vinegar
or lemon juice will
keep fruit better.
Better made the day
of use

Coke Salad

2 Boxes Cherry Jello
1 Large Pineapple (Drained) Chopped
1 Can Bing Cherries Chopped
1 3 Ounce Cream Cheese Mashed
1 Cup Nuts
2 Cakes

Directions:

Heat juice from pineapples and cherries. Pour over jello. Cool. Add cake.
When it begins to thicken fold in nuts fruits and cheese.

Coke Salad   Food

2 Boxes cherry Jello
1 lg. pineapple (drained) Chopped
1 can Bing cherries chop-
1 3oz cream cheese mashed
1 cup nuts
2 cakes -
Heat juice from pin + cher. pour over
jello - Cool add cake - When it begins
to thicken foed in nuts fruit + cheese

Cranberry Salad by Estelle Witherspoon

2 Cups Chopped Cranberries
2 Cups Sugar
2 Cups Hot Water
2 Packages Raspberry Jello
1 1/4 Cup Pineapple Juice
2 Cups Crushed Pineapple Drained
1 Cup Chopped Nuts
2 Cups Chopped Celery

Directions:

Combine cranberries and sugar. Let set. Mix water, jello and pineapple juice. Combine jello with cranberry mix. Add in cranberries, nuts and celery. Refrigerate.

Cranberry Salad by Jerry Springer

3 Ounces Orange Jello
3 Ounces Raspberry Jello
16 Ounces Cranberry (Whole)
14 Ounces Can Crushed Pineapple
2 cups Boiled Water

Directions:

Dissolve jello in boiled water. Add cranberry and pineapple with juice.
Add nuts if desired.

Here's what's cookin': Cranberry Salad
Recipe from: Jerry Springer
1 - 3 oz orange jello
1 - Raspberry jello
1 - 16 oz cranberry (whole)
14 - oz can crushed pine
2 cup boiling water
add cranberry + pineapple with juice -
add nuts if desired

Cranberry Salad by Rachel

2 Cups Cranberries
1 Apple Whole
1 Orange Whole
1 Package Cherry Jello
1/2 Cup Water
1 Cup Sugar
1 Cup Nuts

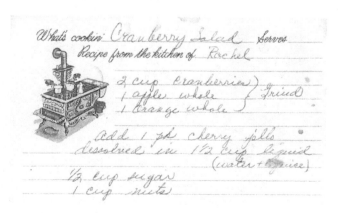

Cranberry Salad by Sarah Posey

1 Box Raspberry Jello
1 Box Cherry Jello
1 Small Pineapple
1 Can Whole Cranberry Sauce
3 Ounces Cream Cheese
Nuts

Directions:

Dissolve jello in 3 cups hot water. Mix in remaining ingredients and refrigerate.

Cranberry Salad — S. Posey
1 Box Rasberry Jello) dissolve in
1 Box Cherry ") 3 cup hot
water
1 Small pineapple
1 Can whole Cranberry Sauce
3 oz. Cream cheese
nuts

Daphine's Fruit Salad

15 1/2 Ounce Chuck Pineapple - Undrained
1 Cup Sugar
1 Egg Beaten
2 Tablespoons All-purpose Flour
1 Cup Pecan Pieces
3 Bananas, Sliced
2 11 Ounces Cans Mandarin Oranges, Chopped
2 Medium Apples, Chopped
1/2 Pound Purple Grapes, Halved and Deeded

Directions:

Drain pineapples, reserving juice. Combine sugar, flour, egg and pineapple juice in small saucepan. Cook over low heat, stirring constantly until smooth and thickened. Cool. Combine pecans and fruit. Add dressing. Stir. Chill.

Daphine's Fruit Salad

1 (15½ oz) can chunk pineapple-undrained
1 cup sugar
1 egg beaten
2 Tbsp. all-purpose flour
1 cup pecan pieces
3 Bananas - sliced
2 (11 oz) cans mandarin oranges (chopped)
2 med. apples - chopped
½ # purple grapes - halved and seeded
(over)

Drain pineapple - reserving juice - Combine
sugar, flour - egg and pineapple juice 'in
small saucepan - Cook over low heat,
stirring constantly, until smooth and
thickened. Cool - Combine pecans and
fruit - Add dressing - Stir - Chill

10-12 Servings

48

Fruit Salad

1 Cup Sugar
1 Egg Beaten
2 Tablespoons Flour
1 Cup Pecan Pieces
3 Bananas, Sliced
2 11 Ounces Mandarin Orange Sections, Drained
2 Medium Apples, Chopped
1/2 Pound Purple Grapes, Halved

Directions:

Drain pineapple, save juice. Combine sugar, flour, egg and pineapple juice.
Cook over low heat. Cool. Add to fruit mix.

1 Cup sugar   Fruit Salad
1 egg beaten   Good
2 Tbs. flour
1 Cup pecan pieces
3 bananas sliced
2 (11 oz) Mandarin Orange sections drained
2 med. apples chopped
1/2 # purple grapes (halved)
Drain pineapple - save juice - Combine
sugar flour egg & Pineapple juice Cook over
low heat Cool - add to fruit mix

49

German Slaw

1 Large Cabbage, Shredded
1 Large Onion, Chopped
1 Large Green Pepper, Chopped
3 Carrots, Grated
1 Cup Sugar
1 Teaspoon Sugar
1/2 Teaspoon Pepper

German Slaw Dressing

1/2 Cup Vinegar
1/2 Cup Oil
2 Teaspoon Sugar
1 Teaspoon Mustard

Directions:

Mix and pour over slaw. Let stand 1 hour in refrigerator. Keeps for 2 weeks.

Green Bean Salad by Nell Herston

1 Can French Style Green Beans, Drained
1 Can Tiny Peas, Drained
1 Can White Corn
1 1/2 Cup Chopped Celery
1 Medium Onion, Chopped
4 Ounce Jar Pimento, Chopped
1/2 Cup Chopped Green Pepper

Green Bean Salad Dressing

3/4 Cup Vinegar
1/2 Cup Oil
1/2 Cup Sugar
1 Teaspoon Salt

Directions:

Mix and pour into salad.

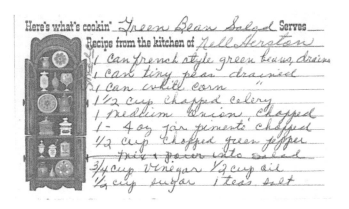

Jello Salad by Sarah

Large Cool Whip
Small Cottage Cheese
Mandarin Oranges, Drained
Small Crushed Pineapple, Drained
1 Package Strawberry Jello

Directions:

Mix together and refrigerate.

Salad   Sarah

Large Cool whip
Small Cottage Cheese
Manadrin oranges   drained
Small crushed pineapple   drained
1 pkg. Strawberry jello

mix together & Ref.

Pistachio Salad

Pistachio Instant Pudding
Small Can Crushed Pineapple
Nuts
Cool Whip
2 Cups Marshmallows

Pistachio Salad

Pistachio Instant Pudding
Sm. can crushed pineapple

nuts.

Cool Whip - 3/4 of 8 oz box
(small)
Marshmellows - 2 cups

Slaw by Sarge's

1 Cup Sugar
1 Cup White Vinegar
1/2 Cup Water
1/2 Cup Oil
1 Head of Cabbage
Onion
Peppers

Directions:

Heat all ingredients. Pour over head of cabbage. Add onions and peppers.

Slaw   Sarge's

Heat 1 c Sugar
     1 c white Vinegar
   1/2 cup water
   1/2 cup oil
Pour over Head of Cabbage –
     add onions & peppers

Strawberry Salad by Rachel Butler

2 Packages Strawberry Jello
1 Large Can Crushed Pineapple
2 10 Ounces Packages Strawberries
3 Very Ripe Bananas, Mashed
1 Cup Nuts
Dash Salt
2 Cartons Sour Cream

Direction:

Drain pineapple and heat juice. Melt jello. Mix fruit and nuts with jello.
Add Salt. Pour 1/2 this in long pan. Let set. Add to top.   Add to top sour
cream. Add other mixture and set in refrigerator.

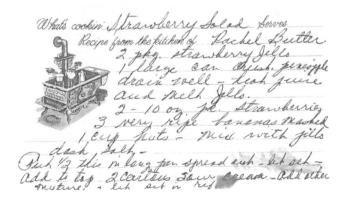

Sweet and Sour Salad by Irene Sneed

1 Large Cabbage, Chopped
1 Green Pepper, Chopped
1 Medium Onion, Chopped
1 Cup Sugar
1 Cup Vinegar
3/4 Cup Vegetable Oil
1 Tablespoon Salt
1 Teaspoon Celery Seed
1 Teaspoon Mustard
1 Teaspoon Turmeric

Directions:

Mix ingredients (exclude cabbage) and bring to boil and pour over cabbage.
Add small amount of turmeric (1 Teaspoon).

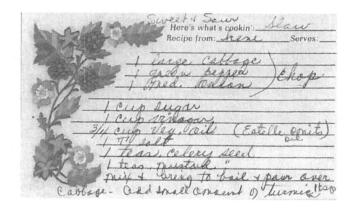

Chapter 2: Sauces and Marinades

Barbeque Sauce by Shirley

3/4 Cup Catsup
3/4 Cup Water
2 Tablespoons Worcestershire Sauce
2 Tablespoons Vinegar
1 Teaspoon Paprika
1 Teaspoon Chili Powder
Salt and Pepper

Barquue Sauce (shirly

3/4 cup catsup
3/4 cup water
2 T Wist. Sauce
2 T vinegar
1 tea. papercia
1 tea. Chili powder
salt + pepper

Celery Seed Dressing by Zelda

1/3 Cup Sugar
1 Teaspoon Salt
1 Teaspoon Dry Mustard
1 Teaspoon Grated Onion
1/4 Cup Vinegar
1 Cup Salad Oil
1 Teaspoon Celery Seed

Directions:

Mix sugar, salt and mustard. Add onion and vinegar. Add oil, 1 tablespoon
at a time, beating constantly with rotary or electric beater until thick. Stir in
celery seed. (This makes 1 1/2 cups and is good for both fruit and
vegetable salads.)

Celery Seed Dressing

1/3 cup sugar   1/4 cup vinegar
1 tsp. salt   1 cup salad oil
1 tsp. dry mustard   1 tsp. celery seed.
1 tsp. grated onion

Mix sugar, salt and mustard; add onion and vinegar.
Add oil, 1 tablespoon at a time, beating constantly
with rotary or electric beater until thick. Stir in
celery seed. (This makes 1 1/2 cups and is good for
both fruit and vegetable salads.)

Zelda

Coleslaw Dressing by Miss Daisy

1/3 Cup Apple Cider Vinegar
1/3 Cup Salad Oil
1/4 Cup Sugar
1 Teaspoon Salt
1/4 Teaspoon Celery Seed
2 Sprigs Parsley, Minced

Directions:

Stir all ingredients until well blended. Pour over slaw. Serve at once.

Here's what's cookin': *Coleslaw dressing*
Recipe from: *Miss Daisy*   Serves:____
1/3 cup apple cider vinegar
1/3 cup salad oil
1/4 cup sugar
1 teas salt
1/4 tea celery seed
2 sprigs parsley minced
Stir all ingredients until well
blended - Pour over slaw &
serve at once

Roquefort Dressing by Miss Daisy

1 Package Sour Cream
1/2 Teaspoon Garlic Salt
1/2 Teaspoon Pepper
1/2 Teaspoon Paprika
1/2 Teaspoon Celery Salt
1 Tablespoon Vinegar
1/2 Cup Mayonnaise
1 Teaspoon Salt
1 Teaspoon Sugar
1/2 Pound Roquefort Cheese, Broken Up

Directions:

Blend all ingredients. Refrigerate 1 day before using.

Soy Sauce Marinade

1/2 Cup Soy Sauce
1/2 Cup Water
2 Tablespoons Lemon Juice
1 Tablespoon Brown Sugar
2 Tablespoons Oil
1/4 Teaspoon Hot Pepper Juice
1 Clove Garlic, Crushed
1/4 Teaspoon Sugar

Directions:

Use on beef or chicken.

Chapter 3: Pickles

Pickle

Drain 1 quart dill pickle and dice. In quart jar, alternate pickle with 2 1/2 cup sugar. Mix with 2 tablespoons pickle spices. Add 2 tablespoons white vinegar. Close tightly. Turn 3 days.

Here's what's cookin':_____
Recipe from:_____ Pickle _____ Serves:____

Drain 1 qt
dill pickle & slice - In
qt. jar alternate pickle
with 2½ C sugar - mix
with 2 T Pickling spice
add - 2 T white vinegar
Close tightly - turn - (3 days)

Pickle with Cucumber and Sugar

Boil and cool:

2 Cup Sugar
1 Cup White Vinegar
8 Cups Cucumber

Add:

1 Cup Chopped Onion
2 Tablespoons Salt
1 Tablespoons Celery Seeds

Directions:

Shake jar often.

Pickle

Boil and Cool
2 cup sugar
1 cup white vinegar
cut up cucumber (8 cups)

add 1 cup chopped onions

add 2T salt
1T. celery seed   shake jar
often —

Squash Pickle by Sarah Posey

8 Cups Squash
2 Cups Sour Cream
4 Peppers
1 Tablespoon Salt
2 Cups Apple Cider Vinegar
3 Cups Sugar
2 Teaspoon Mustard Seed
2 Teaspoons Celery Seed

Directions:

Bring to boil and pour squash over vinegar. Do not boil. Do not cook.

Recipe: Squash Pickle   Yield: ? Sarah
from the kitchen of: _____
8 C. squash
2 C. b. onion) let set 1 hr.
4 peppers
1 T. salt

2 cup apple cider vinegar 3 C. sugar
2 tea mustard seed - 2 tea celery seed

bring to boil - ? pour sq- over
vin - do not boil. do not
cook.

Sweet Pickles by Estelle

2 Cups Limes, pickling
2 Gallons Water, Dissolved
8 Pounds Cucumber, Sliced in 1/2"
1 Tablespoon Whole Cloves
1 Tablespoon Whole Allspice
1 Tablespoon Celery Seed
2 Tablespoons Salt
2 Quarter Vinegar
9 Cups Sugar

Directions:

Pour lime and water over cucumbers. Let stand and soak 24 hours. Tie up cloves, allspice and celery seeds. Mix remaining ingredients together and let stand for 3 hours. Cook all for 15 minutes and can.

RECIPE FOR: Sweet Pickles Estelle
2 cup lime (pickling)
2 gal water - dissolve
Pour over sliced (½") cucumbers
8# - let stand soak 24 hours

Mix 1 T. whole cloves ⟩ 2 qts. Vinegar
1 T " allspice ⟩ Tie up
1 T Celery seed ⟩ 9 cup Sugar
2 T salt - let stand 3 hrs - Cook 15

PREPARATION TIME: _____ SERVES: _____
© LAKE   C.R. GIBSON · NORWALK, CT 06856   Q10-55

67

Chapter 4: Side Dishes

Broccoli by Sarah

1 Package Broccoli, Drained
2 Cups Cooked Rice
1 Can Cream of Chicken Soup
1 Small Jar Cheese Whiz

Baking Instructions:

Bake at 350 degrees for 20 minutes.

Here's what's cookin': Broccoli — Very Good
Recipe from: Sarah   Serves: ____

1 package Broccoli - drained
2 cups cooked rice
1 can cream chicken soup
1 can water chestnuts
1 small jar cheese whiz

Baked   350 - 20 min.

Cheese Ball

8 Ounces Cream Cheese, Room Temperature
1 Cup Sharp Cheese, Graded
1 Tablespoon Onions
3 Drops Tabasco
1 Teaspoon Mustard
1 Teaspoon Worcestershire Sauce
Salt and Pepper

Directions:

Mix well and shape in ball. Refrigerate at least 1 hour.

Corn Pudding by Margie Caruthers

1 Stick Oleo, melted in 8" x 8" Pan
1 Can Corn, Whole Kernel
1 Can Cream Corn
8 Ounces Package Sour Cream
1 Egg
1 Package Corn Muffin Mix

Directions:

Mix and pour in pan.

Baking Instructions:

Bake at 325 degrees for 15 minutes.

RECIPE FOR: Corn Pudding   Margie Caruthers

1 Stick oleo melted in
8"-8" pan -
                              1990
1 can ~~this~~ corn (whole kernel)
1 can cream corn
8 oz. pkg. Sour cream
1 egg
1 tbsp. Corn muffin mix
mix & pour in pan   325-1hr,

PREPARATION TIME: 15 Min.   SERVES: 8
© LAKE   C.R. GIBSON, NORWALK, CT 06856   Q10-55

Fried Okra Patties

1/2 Cup Corn Meal
1/2 Cup Flour
1 Teaspoon Baking Powder
1 1/2 Teaspoon Salt
Pepper to Taste
1/2 Cup Chopped Onion
1 Egg
1/2 Cup Water
1 Pound Okra

Directions:

Combine all ingredients and beat well. Add in okra. Drop by 1 teaspoon in hot oil.

RECIPE FOR: _Fried Okra Patties_
½ C - meal
½ C flour
1 tsp B. Powder
1½ tsp salt - Pepper to taste
½ C chopped onion
1 egg
½ C water - Combine all above
ing and beat well add
1 # Cut okra. Drop by T in hot oil

PREPARATION TIME: _____ SERVES: _____
©LAKE   C.R. GIBSON® NORWALK, CT 06856   Q10-55

Marinated Vegetables

by Barbara Thomas

1 Can Corn
2 Cans French Style Green Beans
1 Can Kidney Beans
1 Can English Peas
2 Ounces Sliced Pimento
1/2 Cup Chopped Celery
1/2 Cup Onion
1 Cup Bell Pepper
1 Cup Sugar
1/2 Teaspoon Pepper
1 Teaspoon Salt
1/2 Cup Oil
3/4 White Vinegar

Directions:

Pour all vegetables in a large colander to drain. Combine remaining
ingredients and stir over medium heat until sugar melts. Cool and pour
over vegetables in an air tight container. Chill for 24 hours.

Marinated Veg.   Barbara Thomas

1 Can Shoe Peg corn
2 "   French Style Green beans
1 "   Kidney beans
1 "   English peas
1-2oz diced pimento
1/2 cup chopped celery
1/2 "   onion
1 cup Bell pepper
Pour all Veg. in a large colander
to drain —   over

    In sauce Pan combine
1 C. Sugar
1/2 tsp pepper
1 tsp salt
1/2 c. oil
3/4 c white vinegar —
"Stir" over med heat until sugar melts
cool - Pour over veg in a air tight
container - Chill 24 hrs. - Keep 2 wks in
refri) Good with Ham, Pork + chicken

Potato Soup by Sarah White

4 Slices Friend Bacon
7 Medium Potatoes, Cut Up
3 Celery Stalks, Chopped
2 Medium Carrots, Chopped
1 Onion, Chopped
4 Cups Water
2 Cups Milk
1 Teaspoon Salt
Pepper to Taste
Parsley
4 Tablespoon Flour

Directions:

Cook vegetables until tender. Add flour and water and add to soup with milk. Cook until thick.

Potato Soup   S. White
4 Slices fried bacon (Remove)
7 med. potatoes - Cut up
3 celery stalks chopped
2 med. carrots   "   (Cook until tender)
1 Onion   "
4 cup water
2 cup milk
1 teas salt + pepper to taste
Parsley   (Mix flour + water - Add
4 T flour   to soup with milk - cook til thick

Squash Casserole

4 or 5 Squash
Onion
1 Cup Cheese
1 Can Cream of Chicken Soup
1 Roll Ritz Crackers, Crushed

Directions:

Cook squash fully. Drain well, combine onion, cheese, cream of chicken and crackers. Put in casserole dish.

Baking Instructions:

Cook for 30-35 minutes at 350 degrees. Sprinkle ritz on top once done.

Squash Casserole

Cook fully, 4 or 5 squash, Drain well, combine onion, + 1 cup Cheese, + one can cream of Chicken soup add 1 roll of ritz Crackers - crushed. Put in Casserole dish. Cook 30-35° @ 350°. Sprinkle ritz on top once done.

Sweet Potato Casserole

3 Cups Hot Sweet Potatoes, Mashed
1/3 Cup Milk
1/2 Cup Oleo
1 Cup Light Brown Sugar
2 Eggs
1 Tablespoons Vanilla

Directions:

Mix and pour in casserole dish.

Sweet Potato Casserole Topping

1 Cup Light Brown Sugar
1 Cup Flour
1/2 Cup Oleo

Directions:

Mix with fork.

Baking Instructions:

Bake uncovered at 350 degrees for 25 minutes.

Sweet Potato Casserole for 10 Servings

3 Cups Mashed Sweet Potatoes
1 Cup Sugar
1/2 Cup Milk
2 Eggs
1 Teaspoon Vanilla

Directions:

Combine and turn into 8 x 10 dish.

Sweet Potato Crumb Mixture

1 Cup Sugar
1/3 Cup Flour
1/3 Cup Oleo
1 Cup Nuts

Directions:

Top on Potatoes.

Baking Instructions:

Bake for 35 minutes at 350 degrees.

Thanksgiving Dressing by Ann Webb

2 Cups Biscuits, Crumbled
2 Cups Cornbread, Crumbled
1/2 Cup Chicken Broth
1 Teaspoon Sage
1/2 Cup Chopped Celery
1/4 Cup Chopped Onion
1/2 Cup Milk
1/4 Cup Melted Oleo

Directions:

Brown bread in cookie sheet. Mix ingredients.

Baking Instructions:

Cook for 1 hour at 350 degrees.

Webb Dressing	⅓ recipe
	brown bread
2 c biscuits (Crumbled)	in cookie sheet
2 c Cornbread (")	Then mix
1½ c chicken broth	ingredients —
1 t. sage	
½ c chopped celery	Cook. 1 hr 350°
¼ c " onion	
½ c milk	
¼ c melted oleo	

Zucchini by Sarah Posey

6 Cups Zucchini, Grated
6 Cups Sugar
Large Crushed Pineapple
2 Packages Small Jello

Directions:

Boil sugar and zucchini for 10 minutes. Add pineapple and boil for 6 minutes. Add jello and stir. Can. Keep refrigerated.

Recipe: Zucchini   Yield: Sarah P.
from the kitchen of: Zucchini
  6 cups grated) boil 10 min.
  6 Cups sugar)

Add lg. crushed pineapple - boil 6 min

Add 2 pk. sm. jello stir + can
Keep R

Chapter 5: Bread

Angel Biscuits by Daphine Caruthers

1 Cup Crisco
5 Cups Plain Flour
2 Packages Yeast
2 Tablespoon Warm Water
1 Tablespoon Sugar
3 Teaspoons Baking Powder
1 Teaspoon Baking Soda
3 Tablespoons Sugar
1 Teaspoon Salt
2 Cups Buttermilk, Room Temperature

Directions:

I put 3 cups of flour in large bowl. Cut in the Crisco. Add other dry ingredients with about 1 cup more flour. Put enough milk to moisten well. Add dissolved yeast and milk. Stir well. Add enough flour to make stiff dough. I put a top on and leave in refrigerator overnight. Roll. Use small cutter. Let set about 10 minutes, then cook.

Baking Instructions:

Bake at 400 degrees for 10 minutes.

84

Angel Cornbread

1 1/2 Cup Corn Meal
1 Package Yeast
1 Tablespoon Sugar
1 Teaspoon Salt
1 1/2 Baking Powder
1 Cup Flour
1/2 Teaspoon Baking Soda
2 Eggs, Beaten
2 Cups Buttermilk
1/2 Cup Oil

Baking Instructions:

Cook at 450 degrees for 10 minutes.

Best Ever Banana Bread

1 3/4 Cups Flour
1 1/2 Cup Sugar
1 Teaspoon Baking Soda
1/2 Teaspoon Salt
2 Eggs
2 Large Ripe Bananas, Smashed
1/2 Cup Oil
1/4 Cup + 1 Tablespoon Buttermilk
1 Teaspoon Vanilla
1 Cup Walnuts

Directions:

Stir or sift together flour, sugar, soda and salt. Mix eggs, bananas, oil, buttermilk and vanilla. Add to flour mixture. Fold in nuts.

Baking Instructions:

Cook at 325 degrees for 1 hour, 20 minutes.

Blueberry Muffins

2 Cups Flour
1/2 Cup Sugar
2 1/4 Teaspoon Baking Powder
1 Teaspoon Salt
1/4 Teaspoon Baking Soda
1 Egg, Slightly Beaten
1 Cup Buttermilk
1/4 Cup Melted Oleo
1 Cup Blueberries

Directions:

Combine dry ingredients in mixing bowl. Set aside. Combine egg,
buttermilk, and butter. Mix well. Make a well in center of dry ingredients.
Pour in liquid ingredients. Stir just until moistened. Fold in blueberries.

Baking Instructions:

Cook at 425 degrees for 25 minutes.

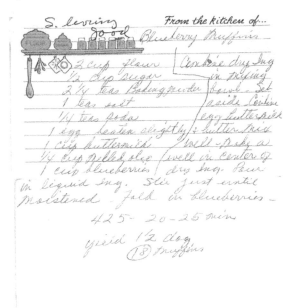

Bran Muffins by Zelda

3 1/2 Cup Nabisco 100% Bran, Separated
1 Cup Boiling Water
1 1/2 Cup Sugar
1/2 Cup Salad Oil
2 Eggs
2 1/2 Cups Flour
1/2 Teaspoon Salt
2 1/2 Teaspoon Baking Soda
2 Cups Buttermilk
1 Cup Raisins or Currants

Directions:

Bring 1 cup bran to boil. Let cool. Mix together sugar, oil, and egg. Add to 2 1/2 cups bran. Sift flour and add to mixture. Add salt and soda, then buttermilk and soaked bran. Add raisins or currants, if desired.

Baking Instructions:

Cook at 400 degrees for 15 - 20 minutes.

Bran Muffins   Zelda   Good
Soak 1 cup Nabisco 100% Bran in
1 cup boiling water - Let cool.

Mix together
1 1/2 cups sugar
1/2 cup salad oil
2 eggs
Add to this - 2 1/2 cups Kellogg All-Bran
Sift together + add
2 1/2 cup flour - 1/2 tsp - salt - 2 1/2 tsp soda

Now add 2 cups buttermilk + the
soaked bran - Mix well.
If desired add 1 cup raisins or
currants.

400° - 15-20 min.

Keep in Ref. 3 weeks

Buttermilk Cornbread

by Daphine Caruthers

1 Cup Corn Meal
1/2 Cup Flour
1/4 Teaspoon Baking Soda
1 Teaspoon Baking Powder
1 Teaspoon Salt
1 Egg, Beaten
1 Cup Buttermilk
1/4 Cup Shortening

Directions:

Heat shortening and pour over mixed bread.

Baking Instructions:

Cook at 400 degrees for 20 minutes.

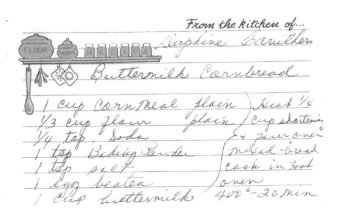

Corn Soufflé by Sarah Posey

1 Stick Oleo, Melted
2 Eggs
8 1/2 Ounces Corn Muffin Mix
8 Ounces Sour Cream
8 Ounces Can Cream Corn, Partially Drained
8 Ounces Whole Kernel Corn, Partially Drained

Directions:

Mix together.

Baking Instructions:

Cook 45 minutes at 350 degrees.

Recipe: Corn Souffle ___ Yield: ___
from the kitchen of: Sarah Posey
1 stick oleo melted
2 eggs
8 1/2 oz corn muffin mix
8 oz S. cream
8 oz can cream Corn   ) partly drain corn
8 oz can whole kernel Corn)
mix together Bake 45 min 350°

Pecan Crescents by Jackie Thurman

1 Cup Butter
1 Cup Nuts, Broken
6 Heaping Tablespoons Powdered Sugar, Sifted
2 1/2 Cups Plain Flour, Sifted
2 Teaspoons Vanilla

Directions:

Melt butter, add flour, sugar, nuts and vanilla. Shape into crescents.

Baking Instructions:

Cook at 350 degrees until brown. Roll in powdered sugar while hot.

Rolls by Daphine Caruthers

5 Cups Flour
1 Yeast
1/2 Cup Water (Warm)
1 Teaspoon Salt
1/4 Cup Sugar
1/4 Cup Lard
2 Cups Water
1 Egg

ROLLS	DAPHINE'S
5 cups flour	2 cups water
1 yeast	1 egg
1/2 cup water(warm)	
1 teaspoon salt	
1/4 cup sugar	
1/4 cup lard	

Chapter 6: Meals

Baked Almond Chicken Salad by Zelda

3 Cup Chopped Cooked Chicken
1 ½ Cup Celery Slices
1 Cup Salad Dressing
½ Cup Toasted Slivered Almonds
1 Cup Grated Swiss Cheese
¼ Cup Onion
2 Tablespoon Chopped Pimento
1 Teaspoon Salt

Directions

Combine all ingredients and enjoy.

Baked Almond Chicken From the kitchen of...
Zelda

3 c chopped chicken
1½ c. celery slices
1 cup salad dressing
½ c toasted slivered almonds
1 c (4 oz) chopped or grated Swiss cheese
¼ c onion
2 T chopped pimento
1 tsp. salt
1 tomato cut in wedge —

Baked Country Ham

Soak in cold water over night.

Pour 16 ounces of Pepsi of Coca Cola over ham.
Add 1 glass of water and cover.

Put in cold over set it to 250 degrees. Leave in over for 3 ½ hours. Turn oven off. Leave ham in oven until completely cooled.

Slice and eat.

Baked Country Ham –

Soak in cold water over night

Pour over Ham 16 oz pepsi or coke
add one glass water – Cover –

Put in cold oven – Set at 250° leave
in oven 3½ hrs – cut oven off – leave
in oven until it completely cook off –
(Slice & eat) Delicious

Broccoli Casserole by Sarah

1 Can Cream of Mushroom Soup
1 Small Can Cheese Whiz
2 Packages Broccoli
1 Package Cauliflower

Directions

Butter baking dish and mix all ingredients.

Baking Instructions

Bake at 350 degrees for 40 minutes.

From the kitchen of... Sarah   Good
broccoli casserole   8-10 serv-
1 can mushroom soup - add
1 small cheese whiz - in
bottom of pan - add
2 pkg broccoli and 1 pkg
cauliflower -   Froz
Tip lid -
40 min   350°
Cheese Casserole

Chicken Casserole by Sarah Posey

8 Ounces Sour Cream
1 Can Cream of Mushroom Soup
½ Can Cream of Chicken Soup
½ Can Celery Soup
6 Chicken Breasts Cut Up
1 Package Crackers with ½ Stick Melted Butter

Directions

Mix all ingredients together. Put cracker mixture in bottom and top of casserole.

Baking Instructions

Bake at 350 degrees until bubbly.

Chicken Casserole   S- Posey
350° - Until Bubble

8 oz Sour Cream
1 Can Mushroom Soup
½ Can Cream of Chicken Soup
½ Can Celery Soup
6 Chicken Breast cut up -
1 pk. Crackers with ½ st. melted oleo
Crush Crackers & put on Top + bottom of pan

Chicken Noodle Soup by Irene Sneed

Onions
Carrots
Celery
Chicken Broth
Milk
Noodles
Chicken

Directions

Cook celery, onion and grated carrots in small amount of water. Add
chicken broth and milk. Let thicken a little. Cook noodles until almost done
and add chicken. Cook until noodles are done.

Chicken Noodle Soup   Irene
Cook Celery
          onions
               grated Carrots in small
    amount of water -
    add chicken broth + Milk.
    thicken a little - Cook noodles
    almost done + add - Cook until
    noodles are done -

Double Cheese Meat Loaf by Miss Daisy

2 8 Ounce Can Tomato Sauce
1 ½ lbs. Ground Beef
½ Cup Cracker Crumbs
1 Teaspoon Salt
½ Cup Chopped Onions
1 Egg
½ Teaspoon Pepper
¾ Cup Grated Mild Cheddar Cheese

Directions

Mix 2/3 of one can of tomato sauce with other ingredients except the cheese. Pour on waxed paper and form rectangle. Put cheese on top. Roll like jelly roll. Place on 9" X 9" dish.

Baking Instructions

Bake at 325 degrees for 1 ½ hours. Then put other tomato sauce on top.

Here's what's cookin': Double-cheese meat loaf
Recipe from: Miss Daisy   Serves: 4
2 - 8 oz cans Tomato sauce   1 egg
        with cheese   ½ tea pepper
1½ # ground beef   ½ tea oregano
½ cup cracker crumbs   ¾ c grated
1 teas salt   mild cheddar cheese
½ cup chopped onion
Heat 325° Mix 2/3 o one can of
tomato sauce with other ing- except
cheese - Pour on waxted paper - form
rectangle. Put cheese on top. Roll
like jelly roll - place on 9'-9' dish
Bake 1 th + 30 min The last 30
minutes - put other Tomato sauce on
                                    top

Dumplings

1 Cup Flour
½ Teaspoon Baking Powder
½ Teaspoon Salt
2 Tablespoon Melted Shortening
½ Cup Milk

Directions

Drop in hot chicken broth. Boil 15 minutes. Do not stir or uncover.

Recipe: Douplins   Yield:
from the kitchen of:
1 C - Flour
1½ tsp. B. Powder
½ tsp. Salt
2 T. Melted Shortening
½ C milk
Drop in hot broth - boil 15 min.
Do not remove Cover

Dumplings Cooked in Chicken Broth

by Nita

1 Cup Flour
1 ½ Teaspoon Baking Powder
½ Teaspoon Salt
2 Tablespoon Melted Shortening
½ Cup Milk

Directions

Combine all ingredients. Drop in hot chicken broth. Cook for 15 minutes. Do not stir.

Dumplings   Nita Peden

1 C flour   Drop in hot
1½ tsp. B. Powder   chicken broth
½ tsp Salt   cover. cook
2 T - melted Shortening) 15 min - Do not
½ cup milk -   stir nor remove cover.

nitas dumplings —   1½ T shortening
2 cup plain flour   Ice water or
1 cup Self-Rising flour Chic. broth

Lasagna by Irene Sneed

Meat Mixture

1 ½ Lbs. Ground Beef
1 Clove of Garlic Minced
1 ½ Tablespoons Parsley Flakes
1 Tablespoon Basil
1 ½ Teaspoon Salt
1 Can of Peeled Tomatoes
2 6 oz. Cans Tomato Paste

Cottage Cheese Filling

10 oz. Lasagna Noodles
3 Cups Cottage Cheese
2 Tablespoons Parsley Flakes
2 Beaten Eggs
2 Teaspoons Salt
½ Teaspoon Pepper
¾ Cup Parmesan Cheese
1 Bag of Mozzarella Cheese

Directions

Brown meat slowly. Drain off grease. Add remaining Meat Mixture ingredients and simmer uncovered for 30 minutes to blend flavor. Cook noodles in boiling water. Drain and rinse in cold water. Combine Cottage Cheese Filling ingredients. Grease pan. Layer noodles, cheese mixture then meat. Repeat.

Baking Instructions

Bake at 375 degrees for 30 minutes then top with mozzarella cheese. Let set for 15 minutes. Enjoy.

Here's what's cookin': Lasagna

Recipe from: Irene   Serves: 6-8

1/2 # beef
1 clove garlic - minced
1/2 Tbs. parsley flakes
1 Tbs. Basil
1 1/2 teas salt
1 - lb can peeled tomatoes
2 - 6 oz. cans tomato paste
— 10 oz lasagna noodles
3 cups cottage cheese
2 Tbs. parsley flakes
2 beaten eggs
2 teas salt — 1/2 teas pepper
1# mozzarella cheese - 3/4 C. parmesan chee

Brown meat slowly - spoon excess
fat. Add next 6 ing. Simmer uncovered
30 min. to blend flavor. Stir cooked
noodles in boiling water - Drain - Rinse
in cold water - Combine cheeses (not
mozzarella) eggs + seasonings -
Grease 13 - 9 - 2 - dish - Layer noodles -
next - cottage cheese mixture - mozzarella
cheese - meat - then Repeat not mozzarella - Bake
375 - 30 min. then add remaining
mozzarella cheese on top - Let set 15
min.

Marinade For Tenderloin

1-3 Table Chili Powder
1 Teaspoon Salt
¼ Teaspoon Ginger
¼ Teaspoon Thyme
¼ Teaspoon Pepper

Directions

Mix all ingredients together. Rub on 2 tenderloins. Cover and refrigerate 2-4 hours. Cook on grill 15 minutes on each side.

Marinade for tenderloin
1-3 T chili Powder
1 teas. salt
¼ teas ginger
¼ " thyme
¼ " pepper
mix together

Rub on two tenderloins — Cover
and Ref. 2-4 hours. Cook on grill
15 min - each side

Meat Loaf

1 Lb Hamburger
1 Medium Chopped Onion
1 Egg
Salt and Pepper
½ Cup Oats or Dry Bread Crumbs
¼ Tomato Sauce
2 Tablespoon Sugar
¾ cup Water
4 Ounces Tomato Sauce
2 Tablespoon Mustard
1 Tablespoon Vinegar

Directions

Mix first 6 ingredients and form meat loaf. Mix remaining ingredients and pour over meat loaf once cooked.

Baking Instructions

Bake at 300 degrees until done.

Meat loaf

Mix 6 ing. + form
1# Hamburger
1 med. Onion Chopped
1 egg
Salt + pepper
⅓ cup Oats or dry crumbs
¼ C tomato sauce
2 T sugar
¾ C Water
4 oz Tomato Sauce   2 T mustard - 1 T Vinegar

meat loaf - mix together other ing + pour loaf - Last while cooking

300° until done

Pizza

Mix
1 Small Can Tomato Sauce
1 Can Tomato Paste
2 Cloves Garlic, Minced
1-2 Teaspoon Oregano
1-2 Teaspoon Basil
1 ½ Teaspoon Salt
Dash of Red Pepper

Dough
1 Tablespoon Oil
3 Cups Flour
1 Cup Warm Water
1 Egg, Beaten
½ Teaspoon Salt
1 Teaspoon Sugar
1 Package Yeast

Directions

Dissolve yeast in warm water. Add 1 ½ cups flour, salt and sugar and mix until smooth. Add egg and oil and beat until glossy. Add enough of remaining flour to make a soft dough. Knead for 6-8 minutes. Put in greased bowl and let rise until doubled in size.

Baking Instructions

Bake at 400 degrees until golden brown.

Here's what's cookin': Pizza
Recipe from: _____ Serves: ___

Mix –
1 Can Tomato Sauce Small
1 " " paste,
2 minced garlic,
1-2 tsp oregano
1-2 tsp basil
1½ tsp salt – dash red pepper
Dough
1 T. Oil – 3 cup flour
1 C warm water – 1 egg beaten
½ tsp salt – 1 tsp sugar
1 pkg yeast.
Dissolve yeast in warm water
Add 1½ cup flour – salt & sugar
and beat until smooth – add
egg + oil and beat until glossy
Add enough remaining flour
to make a soft dough – Knead
6-8 min – Put in greased bowl
& let rise until doubled. Punch
down + refrigerate until ready
To use
Add sausage – cheese to make pizza

107

Rice Casserole

1 Stick butter, Melted
1 Can Cream of Mushroom Soup
2 Can Cream of Chicken Soup
1 Onion
1 Green Pepper
1 Precooked Rice

Directions

Melt one stick of butter. Add mushroom soup and chicken soup with rice.

Baking Instructions

Bake at 350 degrees for 35-40 minutes.

Here's what's cookin': *Rice Casserole*

Recipe from: *Obelene*

Melt 1 stick butter
Add 1 can mushroom
soup - 2 cans chicken soup
with rice soup
1 Onion
1 Green pepper,
1 cup precooked rice
Cook 35-40 min.
350°

Roast

3-4 lb. Roast
½ Cup Strong Black Coffee
½ Cup Soy Sauce
1 Tablespoon Vinegar
1 Tablespoon Worcestershire Sauce
1 Large Onion, Chopped

Directions

Put tenderizer on both sides of roast. Turn roast often in the sauce. Cook in saucepan and make a gravy.

From the kitchen of...

Roast —

3 - 4# Roast — Put tenderizer on both sides turn Roast often in the sauce —
½ cup strong black coffee
½ " Soy Sauce
1 T Vinegar
1 T Wis - sauce
1 large onion chopped
cook in Sauce + make gravy

Sauce For Sweet Potatoes

1 Cup Water
¼ Cup Brown Sugar
¼ Cup White Sugar
¼ Oleo
2 Tablespoon flour

Directions

Combine all ingredients.

Sauce for Sweet Potatoes
Frozen Patties

1 Cup Water (8) 8 times
each
¼ cup B. Sugar (2) to
make
¼ " W " (2) a
gel
¼ oleo — Dash Salt (2) Sticks oleo
2 T flour (16 T) flour
Serves:

Texas Chili

1 ½ Lbs. Ground Beef
1 Medium Onion, Chopped
1 Medium Green Pepper, Chopped
1 Clove Garlic, Minced
3-15 ½ Ounce Cans Small Red Beans, Un-drained
2-6 Ounce Hunts Tomato Paste
1-2 Tablespoon Chili Powder
2 Teaspoon Salt

Directions

In large skillet brown beef, onion, green peppers and garlic. Drain fat from beef. Stir in remaining ingredients, simmer uncovered for 30 minutes.

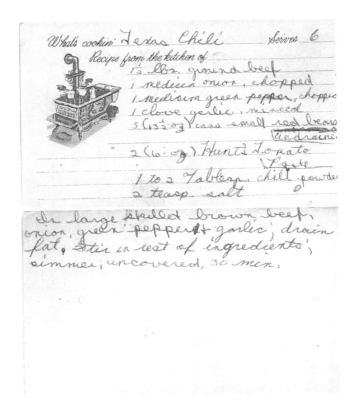

Chapter 7: Desserts

Apple Cake by Nell Ray

2 Cups Sugar
1 ¼ Cups Oil
3 Eggs
1 Teaspoon Vanilla
3 Cups Flour
1 Teaspoon Salt
1 Teaspoon Baking Soda
1 Tablespoon Cinnamon
1 Cup Nuts
3-4 Apples, Chopped
1 Cup Coconut
1 Stick Oleo
1 Cup Brown Sugar
¼ Cup Pet Milk

Direction

Mix sugar, oil, eggs and vanilla. Sift flour, salt, baking soda. Combine remaining ingredients and bake.

Baking Instructions

Bake at 325 degrees for 45 minutes.

RECIPE FOR: Apple Cake   Nell Ray

2 cup sugar
1/4 cup oil
3 eggs
2 teas. Vanilla) mix
3 cup flour
1 teas. Salt) Sift   45 min.
1 " Soda   325°
                           flat pan
1 Tabl. cinnamon — 1 cup nuts)
3-4 apples chopped — 1 cup coconut

PREPARATION TIME: _____ SERVES: _____
© LAKE   C.R. GIBSON® NORWALK, CT 06856   — over —   Q10-55

1 stick oleo
1 cup Brown Sugar) melt
add 1/4 cup pet milk)
   boil 1 minute + pour on cake

115

Apple Cake by Bobby Jean

1 ½ Cup Wesson Oil
1 ½ Cup Sugar
1 Teaspoon Cinnamon
1 Teaspoon Vanilla
3 Large Eggs
2 Cups Flour
1 Teaspoon Salt
1 Teaspoon Baking Soda
1 Cup Nuts
1 Teaspoon Baking Powder
3 Chopped Apples

Directions

Cream oil, sugar, cinnamon, vanilla and eggs. Sift flour, salt and baking soda. Add baking powder and apples to oil mixture. Add nuts. Pour in 9x13 pan.

Baking Instructions

Bake at 350 degrees for 50-60 minutes.

Apple Dumplings

1 ¼ Cup Sugar
1 Tablespoon Cornstarch
1 Stick Oleo
2 Cups Water

Directions

Make pie crust. Cut into squares and fill with apples. Pinch together edges. Place in pan. Mix together sugar, cornstarch, oleo and water and bring to boil. Then pour over baked dumplings.

Baking Instructions

Bake at 350 degrees for 40-45 minutes or until brown. Then after mixture is poured on bake for additional 15 minutes.

350°

Apple Dumplings
make pie crust - cut in squares + fill
with apples - pinch together Place in pan
and bake 40-45 min or until brown.
boil together 1¼ C. Sugar - 1 T
cornstarch - 2 C - water - 1 stick oleo
pour over cobbler + cook about
15 min. longer

Apple Orange Brownies

by Marie Beckham

6 Tablespoons Margarine or Butter
1 Cup Brown Sugar
½ Cup Applesauce
1 Teaspoon Shredded Orange Peel
1 Egg, Beaten
1 Teaspoon Vanilla
1 ¼ Cup Sifted Flour
1 Teaspoon Baking Powder
½ Teaspoon Salt
¼ Teaspoon Baking Soda
½ Walnuts

Directions

In sauce pan combine butter and sugar. Cook until melted. Beat in applesauce, orange peel, egg and vanilla. Sift dry ingredients and stir mixture in saucepan. Add nuts. Create Orange Glaze if desired.

Orange Glaze

1 ½ Cup Confectioners' Sugar
½ Teaspoon Vanilla
Dash of Salt
2 Tablespoons Orange Juice

Baking Instructions

Bake at 350 degrees for 15 minutes.

Apple - Orange Brownies

Marie Beckham

6 T. Marg or Butter
1 C. Brown sugar
½ C. Applesauce
1 t. Shredded Orange peel
1 egg - beaten
1 Teas. Vanilla
1¼ C. Sifted flour
1 t. Baking powder
½ t. Salt - ¼ t Soda   ½ C Walnuts

15½" × 10½"
1" pan

In saucepan combine butter - Sugar. Cook until melted - Beat in applesauce - Orange peel - egg and Vanilla - Sift dry Ing. + stir mixture in saucepan - Add nuts - 350 - 15 min -
Top with orange glaze

Orange Glaze
1½ cups Sifted Conf. Sugar
½ teas Vanilla
Dash Salt
2 T Orange juice

Can be doubled but cook in same pan - 25-30 min double Glaze

119

Banana Pudding

½ Cup Sugar
1/3 Cup Flour
Dash of Salt
4 Eggs, Separated
2 Cups Milk
½ Teaspoon Vanilla
5-6 Bananas
35-40 Vanilla Wafers

Directions

Combine all ingredients to create custard.

RECIPE FOR: _Banana Pudding_
½ C sugar
⅓ C flour
dash of salt
4 eggs (separated)
2 Cup milk
½ t. vanilla

5-6 Bananas
35-40 Wafers

End with Custard

PREPARATION TIME: _____ SERVES: _____
© LAKE   C. R. GIBSON® NORWALK. CT 06856   Q10 55

Butter Pecan Ice Cream by Wilma Polk

1 Cup Packed Brown Sugar
1 Cup White Sugar
1 Can Eagle Brand Milk
1 Quart Half and Half
2 Large Cans Carnation Milk
1 Tablespoon Butter Flavoring
1 Teaspoon Vanilla
1 ½ Cups Toasted Pecans (5 Minutes at 350 Degrees)

Directions
Mix all ingredients and place in freezer. Finish by filling the remaining space of the can with whole milk.

Carrot Cake

1 ½ Cup Wesson Oil
1 ½ Cup Sugar
2 ½ Tablespoons Hot Water
3 Egg Yolks
1 Cup Grated Carrots
3 Cup Flour
1 ½ Teaspoon Cinnamon
1 Teaspoon Nutmeg
1 Teaspoon Allspice
1 Teaspoon Baking Powder
½ Teaspoon Baking Soda
¼ Teaspoon Salt
1 Cut Ground Nuts

Directions

Fold in 3 beaten egg whites. Pour in greased and floured tube pan.

Baking Instructions

Bake at 350 degrees for 1 hour.

Icing

1 Cup Sugar
1 Cup Orange Juice
1 Box Coconut

Directions

Mix ingredients and pour over cake.

"Carrot" Cake

mix
1½ C wesson oil
1½ C sugar
2½ Tbsp hot water   1 tsp allspice
3 egg yolks   1 tsp Baking powder
1 C grated carrots   ½ tsp Baking soda
2 C flour   ¼ tsp salt.
1½ cinnamon   1 C nuts ground
1 tsp nutmeg
                           (over)

fold in 3 Beaten egg whites
pour in greased & flowered tube pan
    Bake 1 hour at 350
         (cool)

      Icing
1 C sugar
1 C orange
1 Box coconut or can put on cake
and pour mixture of juice & sugar slowly
                              over cake

123

Chocolate Cake by Virginia Woodard

1 ¾ Cup Sugar
1 Stick Oleo
2 ½ Cup Flour
¾ Cup Buttermilk
2 Level Teaspoons Baking Soda (In Milk)
2 Eggs
½ Cup Cold Water
½ Cup Cocoa
1 Teaspoon Vanilla
Dash of Salt

Directions

Combine all ingredients and bake.

Baking Instructions

Bake at 350 degrees for 30 minutes.

Chocolate Cake   V. Woodard
1 3/4 C. Sugar
1 St. oleo
2 1/2 cup flour
3/4 cup buttermilk
2 level teas soda (in milk)
2 unbeaten egg
1/2 cup cold water
1/3 cup cocoa
1 teas vanilla
salt   oven 350° 30 min

Chocolate Sheet Cake

1 Cup Oleo
¼ Cup Cocoa
1 Cup Water
2 Cups Unsifted Flour
1 ½ Cups Packed Brown Sugar
1 Teaspoon Baking Soda
1 Teaspoon Cinnamon
½ Teaspoon Salt
1 Can Eagle Brand Milk
2 Eggs
1 Teaspoon Vanilla
1 Cup Cornstarch
1 Cup Chopped Nuts

Directions

Melt 1 cup oleo. Stir in ¼ cup cocoa then add water. Bring to boil. Remove.
In large mixer bowl combine flour, sugar, baking soda, cinnamon and salt.
Add cocoa mixture. Add 1/3 cup eagle brand milk, eggs and vanilla. Pour in
15 x 10 pan.

Make Spread
In small pan melt ¼ cup oleo. Stir in ¼ cup cocoa and eagle brand milk.
Stir in sugar and nuts. Spread over warm cake.

Baking Instructions

Bake at 350 degrees for 15 minutes.

Choc. Sheet Cake

1 Cup oleo
1/4 Cup Cocoa
1 Cup water
2 " unsifted flour
1 1/2 cups packed brown sugar
1 teas. Soda
1 " cinnamon
1/2 " salt
1 Can Eagle Brand milk
2 eggs

1 teas Vanilla
1 Cup Con. Sugar
1 " chopped nuts

350°

Melt 1 cup oleo - Stir in 1/4 cup cocoa then water - Bring to boil - Remove. In large mixer bowl combine fl. Sugar - Soda cin + salt. Add Cocoa mixture - Stir in 1/3 cup Eagle Brand, eggs + Vanilla Pour in 15 × 10" Jellyroll pan - Bake 15 min

In small pan - melt oleo 1/4 C oleo - Stir in 1/4 C cocoa + Eagle Brand - Stir in Sugar + nuts - Spread on warm Cake

Cobbler by Irene Sneed

1 Stick Oleo, Melted In Pan
4 Cups Fruit
1 Cup Sugar, Divided (1/2 For Fruit and ½ For Flour)
¾ Cup Flour
2 Teaspoon Baking Powder
¾ Cup Milk

Directions

Mix all ingredients together. Pour Mixture over butter. Do not stir. Place in baking pan.

Baking Instructions

Bake at 350 degrees for 55 minutes.

Recipe: _Cobbler –_ Yield: _Irene_
from the kitchen of: _____ 350° 55 min.

1 Stick oleo melted in pan (pour mixture over butter- do not stir)

4 cup fruit
1 cup sugar (divided) ½ fruit ½ flour
3/4 c flour
2 t. Baking Powder – 3/4 c milk

Coconut-Carrot Cake

1 ¾ Cup Flour Unsifted
2 Teaspoon Baking Soda
2 Teaspoon Cinnamon
1 Teaspoon Salt
2 Cup Sugar
1 ½ Cup Oil
4 Large Eggs
2 Teaspoons Vanilla
2 Cups Shredded Carrots
1 8 Ounce Can Pineapple
1 Cup Coconut
1 Cup Pecans
½ Cup Golden Raisins

Directions

Combine all ingredients and prepare to bake.

Baking Instructions

Bake at 350 degrees for 30 minutes.

Coconut - Carrot Cake
1¾ c flour unsifted
2 t. soda
2 t. cin.   1 cup coconut
1 t. salt   1 cup pecans
2 cup sugar   ½ cup golden raisen
1½ cup oil.
4 lg. eggs   35° - 30 min.
2 t. vanilla   3 sq. pans
2 c. shredded carrots
1 can 8 oz crushed pineapple

Coconut Pound Cake

2/3 Cup Crisco
2 Sticks Oleo
3 Cups Sugar
3 Cups Plain Flour
1 Teaspoon Baking Powder
1 Cup Milk
1 Cup Coconut (Packed)
5 Eggs
1 ½ Teaspoon Coconut Flavoring

Directions

Cream sugar, shortening and oleo. Add eggs one at a time. Beat well after each. Add flour and baking powder all at once. Add flavoring, milk and coconut. Mix well.

Baking Instructions

Bake at 325 degrees for 1 ½ hours in Bundt pan.

Coconut Pound Cake
2/3 Cup Crisco
2 sticks Oleo
3 cups Sugar
3 cups Plain flour
1 tsp baking powder
1 cup milk   Sometimes we
1 cup Coconut (Packed) more   use
5 eggs
1 1/2 tsp coconut flavour
Cream) gar, shortening together (?)

Add eggs one at a time. Beat
well after each. Add flour
baking powder all at one time.
Add flavoring, milk then Coconut
Beat well. Bake 1 1/2 hours
at 375° in Bundt Cake Pan.

Date Nut Balls

1 Stick Oleo
1 Cup Sugar
1 Egg
1 8 Ounce Box Dates
½ Cup Nuts

Directions

Add nuts and pour over 4 cups rice krispies. Mix well and let cool and form into balls. Roll in powdered sugar.

date nut Balls

1 stick oleo
1 cup sugar   cook 6 to 8 min
1 egg
1 - 8oz box dates
½ cup nuts

Add nuts and pour over 4 c. Rice
Krispies. Mix well - Let cool & shape in
balls - Roll in cocoanut or powdered Sugar

Devil's Food Cake by Miss Daisy

1 Cup Butter
2 ½ Cups Sugar
5 Eggs
2 ½ Cups Flour
1 Teaspoon Baking Soda
1 Cup Buttermilk
4 Ounces Bitter Chocolate, Melted
3 Teaspoons Vanilla

Directions

Cream butter add one cup sugar gradually. Then add the rest of the sugar. Add the eggs one at a time then beat well. Add the baking soda to buttermilk. Alternate adding the flour and buttermilk. Add the chocolate and vanilla and create 3 layers. Add to 9" layer pan.

Baking Instructions

Bake at 350 degrees for 25 minutes.

Here's what's cookin': Devils Food Cake
Recipe from: Miss Daisy   Serves:____

1 cup butter   1 cup Buttermilk
2½ cup sugar   4 ozs Bitter choc.
5 eggs   melted
2½ cup flour   3 teas Vanilla
1 teas soda
Preheat oven 350° - Cream butter add.
1 cup sugar gradually - Then rest g sugar.
add egg one at time - beat well - add
soda to milk. add flour + milk
alternate. - add choc. + vanilla
3 layers - 9" layer pans.
about 25 min.

Easy Fruit Cake by Sarah Posey

2 Cups Chopped Dates or 1 Cup Cherries
½ Cup Cherries
½ Cup Pineapples
1 ½ Cup Chopped Nuts
1 Can Coconut
1 Can Eagle Brand Milk

Directions

Combine all ingredients.

Baking Instructions

Bake at 300 degrees for 1 hour in long log pan.

Fudge Cake by Shirley

2 Cups Sugar
1 Cup Wesson Oil
4 Eggs Separated
2 Cups Flour
1 Teaspoon Baking Powder
½ Teaspoon Salt
3 Ounces Chocolate Melted in ½ Cup Hot Water
1 Cup Milk
2 Teaspoon Vanilla

Directions

Sift flour, baking powder, and salt together. Combine all ingredients to form batter.

Baking Instructions

Bake at 325 degrees for about 1 hour.

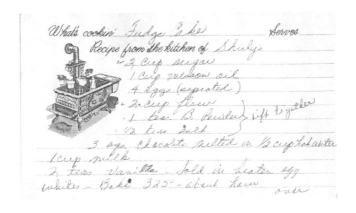

Glaze

1/3 Cup Oleo
2 Cups Confectioner Sugar
1/3 Teaspoon Cinnamon
3-4 Tablespoon Apple Juice or Cider

Directions

Mix together ingredients.

Gumdrop Bars by Irene Sneed

2 Cups Sifted Flour
¼ Teaspoon Salt
1 Teaspoon Cinnamon
3 Eggs, Beaten
2 Cups Brown Sugar
¼ Cup Evaporated Milk
1 Cup Soft Gumdrops, Cut
½ Cup Chopped Nuts

Directions

Sift together flour, salt and cinnamon then combine remaining ingredients.

Baking Instructions

Bake at 325 degrees for 35 minutes.

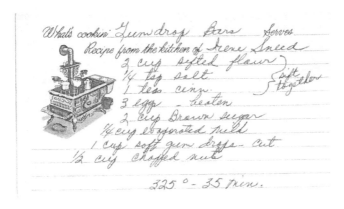

Refrigerator Dessert by Mary Dale

1 Cup Flour
½ Cup Pecans
1 Stick Butter
1 Tablespoon Sugar
8 Ounces Cream Cheese
1 Cup Powdered Sugar
1 Cup Cool Whip
2 Packages Chocolate Pudding
2 ¾ Cups Milk

Directions

Mix flour, pecans, butter and sugar. Press in flat dish. Bake at 350 degrees for 15 minutes. Let cool. Second layer. Mix cream cheese, powdered sugar and cool whip. Third layer. Chocolate pudding packages and milk. Mix and create layer. Fourth layer. Top with remaining cool whip and pecans.

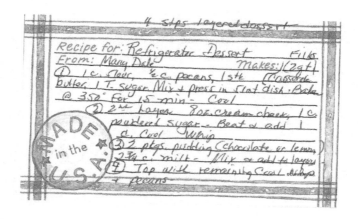

Roasted Pecans by Sarah Posey

4 Cups Pecan Halves
2 Tablespoons Butter
2 Teaspoon Worcestershire Sauce
Dash of Tabasco Sauce
½ Teaspoon Salt

Directions

Sauté pecans in butter and the add other ingredients.

Baking Instructions

Bake at 325 degrees for 20 minutes.

Roasted Pecans
S- Posey
1 # (4 cup) pecan halves
2 T butter
2 t. Worchestershire Sauce
Dash Tabasco Sauce
½ t Salt
Saute pecans in butter add other
Ing. Bake 20 min — 325°

Spiced Peaches

1 Can Peach Halves
¾ Cup Packed Brown Sugar
½ Cup White Vinegar
1 Tablespoon Whole Pickle Spice

Directions

Drain peaches. Boil sugar, vinegar and spice. Add to peaches.

Spiced Peaches

1 (2½) can, Halves
¾ Cup B. Sugar (Packed)
½ cup white Vinegar
1 T whole pickle spice

drain Peaches
boil mixture then add
the Peaches -   Ref—

Chapter 8: Frostings

Buttermilk Frosting

by Claudia Caruthers

1/4 Cup Cocoa
1/2 Cup Butter, Cubed
1/2 Cup Buttermilk
3 3/4 Cup Confectioner's Sugar
1 Teaspoon Vanilla
1/2 Cup Pecans, Chopped

Directions:

Bring cocoa, butter and buttermilk to a boil. Whisk in sugar and sugar.
Spread on warm cake. Sprinkle nuts on top.

Caramel Icing by Sarah White

1 Stick Oleo
2 Cups Brown Sugar
1/2 Cup Evaporated Milk
1 Teaspoon Vanilla
1 Box Powdered Sugar

Directions:

Melt oleo and add brown sugar and boil 2 minutes. Add milk and bring to boil. Add vanilla and cool. Add confectioner's sugar (about a box) enough to spread on cake.

S. White

Caramel Icing

1 Stick oleo (Can use 1½ sticks oleo - I
do not
2 cup Brown Sugar
Melt oleo and add sugar + boil
2 minutes -
add ½ cup evap. milk + bring to boil
1 teas. Vanilla - Cool and add
Conf. (Powdered) sugar enough to
spread on Cake - (Takes about 1 Box

Caramel Icing by Virginia Woodard

3 Cups Sugar, Separated
1 cup Milk or Cream
7 Marshmallows
1 Teaspoon Vanilla

Directions:

Butter skillet. Brown 1 cup of sugar. Low heat 2 cups sugar and 1 cup milk in pan to get hot. Pour milk mixture over browned sugar. Test. Soft boil. Add marshmallows and vanilla.

What's cookin' Carmel Icing   Serves
Recipe from the kitchen of Virginia Woodward
3 Cup sugar
1 cup milk or cream
7 Marshmallows
1 tsp Vanilla

Butter skillet -
brown 1 cup of the sugar. low heat
2 cup sugar + 1 cup milk in pan - to get
hot - pour milk mixture over browned
sugar - test - soft boil - add marsh + Vanilla

Chocolate Icing by Jackie Thurman

2 Cups Sugar
1 Stick Oleo
1/2 Cup Milk
1/4 Cup Karo
Dash Salt
3 Teaspoons Cocoa
1 Teaspoon Vanilla

Directions:

Let simmer until butter and sugar melt. Boil hard for one minute. Take off
and add vanilla.

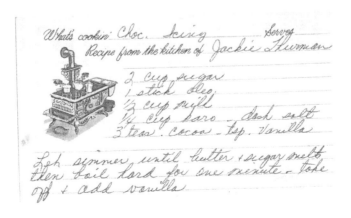

Cream Cheese Frosting

8 Ounces Cream Cheese
1/2 Cup Oleo
1 Teaspoon Vanilla
3/4 Cup Confectioner's Sugar
1/4 Teaspoon Cinnamon

Directions:

Heat with electric beaters.

RECIPE FOR: _Cream cheese frosting_

2½ pkg. (8 oz) cream cheese
½ cup oleo
1 tsp. vanilla
3/4 c. conf. sugar
1/4 tsp. cinn.

beat with elec. beaters

PREPARATION TIME: _____ SERVES: _____
© LAKE   C.R. GIBSON® NORWALK, CT 06856   Q16·55

Icing For German Chocolate Cake

1 12 Ounce Can Evaporated Milk
1 ½ Cup Sugar
¾ Cup Butter (1 ½ Sticks)
4 Egg Yolks, Beaten
1 ½ Teaspoon Vanilla
2 2/3 Cup Coconut
1 ½ Cups Pecans

Directions

Cook milk, sugar, butter, egg yolks until brown. Mix in remaining ingredients.

Recipe: *Icing for* German Choc. Cake   Yield: _____
from the kitchen of: _____
1 - 12 oz evaporated Milk   Cook until
1½ C. Sugar   Brown +
3/4 C. butter (1½ Sticks)   thick - about
4 egg yolk (Beaten)   12 min.
1½ teas. vanilla
1 - 7 oz coconut (2 ⅔ c)
1½ cup pecans

Oreo Icing

2 Cups Sugar
2 Tablespoons Cocoa
½ Cup Milk
2 Tablespoons Syrup
1 Stick Oleo

Directions

Mix all ingredients and cook 1 ½ - 2 minutes on soft boil. Add vanilla to taste.

Icing
2 cup sugar
2 T cocoa
1/2 c. milk
2 T syrup
1 stick oleo -
Cook 1/2 to 2 min - Soft ball
Add Vanilla

Vanilla Sauce

1/2 Cup Sugar
1 Tablespoon Flour
1 Cup Water
1 Teaspoon Vanilla
1 Tablespoon Oleo

Directions:

Let boil and leave on burner until cool.

RECIPE FOR: _Vanilla Sauce_

½ c. Sugar
1 T. Flour
1 C. Water
1 t. vanilla
1 T. oleo

Let boil – and leave on burner
until cool.

PREPARATION TIME: _____ SERVES: _____
© LAKE   C.R. GIBSON® NORWALK CT 06856   Q10 55

White Icing by Sarah Posey

2 1/2 Cups Sugar
1/2 Cup White Karo
1/2 Cup Water
2 Egg Whites, Beaten
3 Tablespoons Powdered Sugar

Directions:

Cook sugar, karo and water until 242 degrees. Pour over eggs. Add powdered sugar and vanilla.

RECIPE FOR: _White Icing Sarah Po___

2½ c sugar
½ c white karo } Cook
½ c water } 242°

Pour over 2 beaten egg whites - Add
3 T powdered sugar
vanilla

PREPARATION TIME: _____ SERVES: _____
©LAKE   C.R. GIBSON® NORWALK, CT 06856   Q10-55

Chapter 9: Cookies

Cowboy Cookies

1 Cup Shortening
1 Cup Brown Sugar
2 Eggs
2 Cups Plain Flour
1 Cup Granulated Sugar
1 Teaspoon Baking Soda
1/2 Teaspoon Baking Powder
1/2 Teaspoon Salt
2 Cups Oatmeal
1 Teaspoon Vanilla
6 Ounces Chocolate Chips

Here's what's cookin': Cowboy Cookies
Recipe from:_____ Serves:_____
Cream — 1 Cup Shortening
1 cup Brown Sugar

Add — 2 - Eggs -
Sift - 2 - cups plain flour
1 - cup Granulated sugar
1 - tsp Soda
½ tsp baking Powder
½ tsp salt
Add - to mixture -
2 - cups Oatmeal
1 - tsp Vanilla
1 - 6 oz Chocolate chips

Date Nut Ball Cookies by Donna Roland

1 Egg
1 Stick Oleo
1 Cup Sugar
1 8 Ounce Package Dates
1/2 an Coconut
1 1/2 Cup Rice Krispies
1 Cup Pecans
1 Teaspoon Vanilla
Powdered Sugar

Directions:

Cook first 4 ingredients for 10 minutes on medium heat. Stir constantly.
Mix in other ingredients. Cool. Shape into balls and roll in powdered
sugar.

Dish Pan Cookies

2 Cups Oil
2 Cups Sugar
2 Cups Brown Sugar
4 Eggs
4 Cups Flour
2 Teaspoons Vanilla
2 Teaspoons Baking Soda
1 Teaspoon Salt
2 Cups Coconut
2 Cups Corn Flakes
1 1/2 Cups Oatmeal
1 1/2 Cups Salted Peanuts
12 Ounces Chocolate Chips
Nuts

Directions:

Mix well and top by teaspoons.

Baking Instructions:

Bake at 350 degrees for 12 minutes.

RECIPE FOR: Dish Pan Cookies
2 c - Oil
2 C W-Sugar
2 C B- sugar
4 eggs   2 cup Corn flakes
4 cup flour   1½ c Oatmeal
2 tsp Vanilla   1½ C salted peanuts
2 tsp Soda   12 oz choc. chip
1 tsp salt   nuts
2 cup coconut   mix well - drop
PREPARATION TIME: 350° - 12 min SERVES: by teaspoon
© LAKE   C.R. GIBSON,® NORWALK, CT 06856   very stiff Q10 55

Haystacks

2 Packages or 1 Big Butterscotch Morsels
5 1/2 Ounces Canned Chow Mein Noodles
1 Cup Chopped (or Whole) Salted Peanuts

Directions:

Melt butterscotch morsels in top of double boiler over low heat. Add noodles and nuts. Stir lightly till all the noodles are coated. Drop by the spoonfuls onto waxed paper. Let stand until firm.

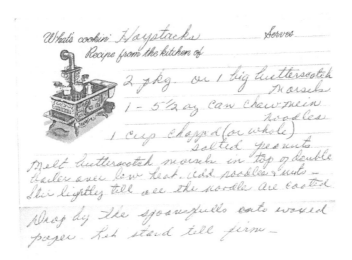

Magic Cookie Bars by Nancy Hunter

1/2 Cup Butter
1 1/2 Cups Graham Cracker Crumbs
1 Can Sweetened Condensed Milk
6 Ounces Semi-Sweet Chocolate Chips
1 Can (3 1/2 Ounce) Flaked Coconut
1 Cup Chopped Nuts

Directions:

In 13 X 9 inch baking pan, melt butter. Remove from heat. Sprinkle crumbs over butter. Pour sweetened condensed milk evenly over crumbs. Top with chocolate chips, coconut and nuts. Press down gently.

Baking Instructions:

Bake at 350 degrees for 25 minutes or until golden brown. Cool. Cut into 3 X 1 1/2 inch bars.

Oatmeal Chipper Cookies

by Daphine Caruthers

1 1/4 Cup Quick Oatmeal
1 Cup Sifted Flour
1/2 Cup Sugar
1/2 Cup Brown Sugar
1 Cup Flaked Coconut
1/2 Cup Semisweet Chocolate Pieces
1/2 Teaspoon Baking Soda
1/2 Teaspoon Salt
1/2 Cup Vegetable Oil
1 Egg
1 Teaspoon Vanilla

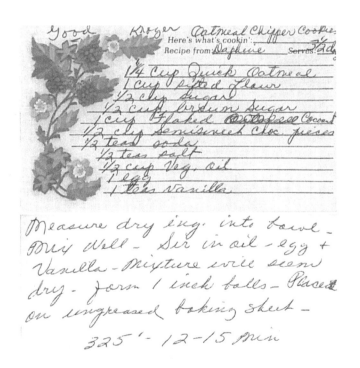

Oatmeal Cookies by Mike Caruthers

1 Cup Brown Sugar
1 Cup Sugar
1 Cup Flour
1 cup Oil
1 Scant Teaspoon Baking Soda
Pinch Salt
4 Cups Oatmeal
2 Eggs, Beaten

Baking Instructions:

Bake at 325 degrees for 15 minutes.

What's cookin' Oatmeal Cookies Serves 60
Recipe from the kitchen of Mike Caruthers

1 cup Brown sugar —
1 cup White sugar
1 cup Flour
1 cup wesson oil
1 scant teas. soda
pinch salt - 4 cup oatmeal
2 whole eggs - beaten

325° - 15 min.

Oatmeal Cookies by Pauline Davis

2 Sticks Butter
1 Cup Brown Sugar
1 Cup Sugar
2 Eggs
2 Cups Self-rising Flour
2 Cups Oats
1 Teaspoon Vanilla
1 Cup Flaked Coconut
1 Cup Chopped Pecans
1 Cup Orange Slices
1 Cup Raisins

Directions:

Combine all. If dough stiff, add small amount of milk or water. Make ball size of large marbles. Press with fork.

Baking Instructions:

Bake at 350 degrees until light brown.

Oatmeal Cookies with Raisons

by Suzy Herston

1 Cup Butter
1 Cup Sugar
2 Eggs, Beaten
1 Tablespoon Milk
3/4 Teaspoon Baking Soda
2 Cups Flour
1/2 Teaspoon Salt
1 Teaspoon Cinnamon
1 Cup Raisons
2 Cups Rolled Oats

Directions:

Cream butter and sugar. Add egg and milk. Sift together dry ingredients and add to egg mixture. Add in remaining ingredients.

Ranger Cookies

1 Cup Oleo
1 Cup Sugar
1 Cup Brown Sugar
2 Large Eggs
2 Cups Cornflakes
2 Cups Oatmeal
2 Cups Flour, Sifted with:
1 Teaspoon Baking Soda
1 1/2 Teaspoon Baking Powder
1 Cup Coconut
1 Teaspoon Vanilla
1 Cup Nuts

Directions:

Bake at 350 degrees for 10 - 12 minutes.

RECIPE FOR: *Cookies   Marton - Ray*
1 cup oleo   *Ranger Cookies*
1 cup W. Sugar
1 " B - "   1 Cup Coconut
2 larg eggs   1 tear Vanilla
2 C = Corn flakes   1 cup nuts
2 C Oatmeal
2 C plain flour sifted with
1 teas Soda
1½ teas Baking Powder   350°
PREPARATION TIME: _____350°_____ SERVES: _____
© LAKE   C R GIBSON * NORWALK CT 06856   Q10-55

Sliced Cookies

1 Pound Vanilla Wafers, Crushed
1 Eagle Brand Milk
1 Cup Nuts
1 Cup Chopped Pecans
1 Cup Chopped Cherries
1/4 Cup Brandy

Sliced Cookies — Food
1# Vanilla Wafers crushed
1 eagle Brandy Brand milk
1 C Nuts
1 C chopped pecans
1 C " Cherries
1/4 cup brandy

Sugar Cookies

1 Cup Powdered Sugar
1 Cup Sugar
1 Cup Oleo
1 Cup Vegetable Oil
2 Eggs, Beaten
4 - 4 1/2 Cups Flour
1 Teaspoon Salt
1 Teaspoon Baking Powder
1 Teaspoon Cream of Tartar
1 Teaspoon Vanilla

Directions:

Chill and roll out or 1 " balls. Roll in sugar. Press down.

Vanishing Oatmeal Cookies

by Jean Johnson

1 Cup Butter
1 Cup Packed Brown Sugar
1/2 Cup Sugar
2 Eggs
1 Teaspoon Vanilla
1 1/2 Cup Flour
1 Teaspoon Baking Soda
1 Teaspoon Cinnamon
1/2 Teaspoon Salt
3 Cups Quick Oats
1 Cup Raisins

Directions:

Mix all ingredients. Add to the first 5 ingredients. Add oats and raisins last.

Baking Instructions:

Bake at 350 degrees for 10 - 12 minutes.

Chapter 10: Pies

Pie Crust

2 Cups Flour
1/2 Teaspoon Salt
1/3 Cup Oleo
1/3 Cup Vegetable Shortening
1/3 Cup Ice Water

Pie Crust
2 C flour
1/2 t Salt
1/3 C Oleo
1/3 C Veg. shortening

Food

ice water 1/3 C about

2 crusts

Pie Crust for Fried Pies

1 Cup Flour
1 Teaspoon Baking Powder
1/4 Teaspoon Salt
3 Tablespoons Shortening
1/3 Cup Cold Milk

Directions:

Mix dry ingredients, then add the milk.

Basic Cream Pie

3/4 Cup Sugar
1/4 Teaspoon Salt
3 Tablespoons Corn Starch
2 Cups Milk
3 Egg Yolks
3 Tablespoons Margarine
1 Teaspoon Vanilla

Directions:

Cook first 4 ingredients in double boiler. Add beaten yolks. Cook 3 minutes. Use wire whisk to ship oleo and vanilla.

See below for additions to Cream Pie.

Here's what's cookin': Basic Cream Pie
Recipe from: _____ Serves: ____
3/4 cup sugar
1/4 teas. salt
3 tea. Corn Starch (3 T)
2 cup milk
3 egg yolks
3 Tablespoon marg.
1 teas. vanilla

Cook first 4 ing. in double boiler - Add beaten yolks cook 3 min. Use wire whisk to whip oleo + vanilla

3 egg whites - Stiff - 1/4 cup sugar and 1 teas vanilla - 325° - 5 - 7 min.

Pineapple Pie - 1/2 cup drained crushed pineapple

Coconut - 1/4 cup coconut

Choc - Use 1 cup sugar and 2 Tablespoon cocoa.

Buttermilk Pie by Laura White

1/2 Cup Oleo
2 1/2 Cup Sugar
1/2 Teaspoon Cinnamon
1 Tablespoon Flour
2 Eggs
1/2 Cup Buttermilk

Directions:

Mix first 4 ingredients. Add one egg at a time, then buttermilk.

Baking Instructions:

Bake at 350 degrees for 10 minutes. Reduce and cook 45 minutes.

Cherry Pie

1 Cup Sugar
2 Tablespoons Cornstarch
¼ Cup Cherry Juice
¼ Teaspoon Red Food Coloring
½ Teaspoon Almond Flavoring
1 #2 Can Cherries, Drained

Directions:

Mix ingredients and pour into unbaked pie shell.

Baking Instructions:

Bake at 350 degrees for 1 hour.

Chess Pie by Missie Hargrove

3 Whole Eggs, Beaten with Fork
1 ½ Cup Sugar
1 Stick of Butter
1 ½ Teaspoon Vinegar
1 Teaspoon Vanilla
1 Heaping Tablespoon Corn Meal

Directions:

Mix ingredients and pour into uncooked pie shell.

Baking Instructions:

Bake at 350 degrees for 25 minutes. Reduce heat if cooking too fast.

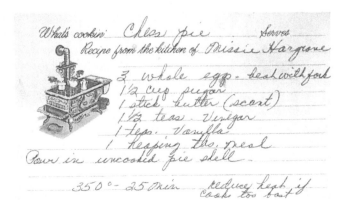

Chocolate Chess Pie

1 ½ Cup Sugar
2 Eggs
3 Tablespoons Cocoa
1 Teaspoons Vanilla
½ Stick Melted Butter
1 Small Can Carnation Milk

Directions:

Mix ingredients and pour into unbaked crust.

Baking Instructions:

Bake at 325 degrees for 45 minutes.

Choc. Chess Pie
1½ cup sugar
2 eggs
3 T. Cocoa
1 teas. Vanilla
½ stick melted butter
1 Sm. can carnation milk

Pour in unbaked crust — 45 min 325°

Freezes well!

Chocolate Pie by Sarah Posey

1 ¾ Cup Sugar
1/3 Cup Flour
¼ Cup Cocoa
2 Cup Milk
4 Large Eggs – Separated
2 Tablespoons Melted Oleo

Directions:

Mix ingredients and pour into heavy pan. Pour into cooked pie shell

Baking Instructions:

Bake at 325 degrees for 25 minutes.

RECIPE FOR: Chocolate Pie
1¾ cup sugar
1/3 cup flour
¼ cup cocoa
2 cups milk
4 large eggs - Separated
2 T. melted olio (cooled)

Egg whites
½ teas cream of tartar

PREPARATION TIME: _____ SERVES: _____

Coconut Pie by Sarah

2 Tablespoon Self Rising Flour
1 ¾ Cup Milk
½ Cup Sugar
2 Egg Yolks
1 Teaspoon Vanilla
1 Tablespoon Butter
1 Cup Coconut

Directions

Mix flour, milk, sugar and egg yolks and cook until thick. Add butter and vanilla then add coconut.

Coconut Pie.   Sarah

2 T. Flour (Self-Rising)
1¾ cup milk
½ cup sugar
2 egg yolk

Mix above + cook until
thick Remove — add 1 T
butter & 1 teas Vanilla — add
Cocoanut — top with egg white.

Come to rolling boil stirring
constantly. When most of sugar has
melted stir well. It should be
caramalized + bubbly all over.
add first mixture + stir constantly
continue cooking until thick +
creamy.

Custard Pie

4 Eggs, Slightly Beaten
½ Cup Sugar
¼ Teaspoon Salt
½ Vanilla
2 ½ Cup Milk (Scalded)

Directions:

Mix ingredients stirring in vanilla gradually. Pour into whole pie shell and sprinkle with nutmeg.

Baking Instructions:

Bake at 350 degrees for 30-4- minutes. Test with knife. Cool on rack.

Custard Pie
4 eggs slightly beaten
½ cup sugar
¼ teas salt
½ teas vanilla — gradually stir in
2½ cup milk (scalded) — pour in unbaked
pie shell. Sprinkle with nutmeg. Bake in
350° - 35-40 min. - test with knife
Cool on rack

French Coconut Pie by Ruth

1 1/3 Cups Sugar
1 Stick of Margarine
3 Whole Eggs
¼ Cup Orange Juice (or Lemon Juice)
Grated Rind of Orange (or Lemon)
1 Teaspoon Vanilla
1 Can Angel Flake Coconut

Directions:

Melt margarine in sauce pan over low heat. When barely melted add sugar and beat. Add whole eggs one at a time. Stir in orange juice, vanilla, rind and coconut. Pour into unheated pie shell.

Baking Instructions:

Bake 30-40 minutes at 325 degrees until firm

French Coconut Pie   Ruth

1 1/2 cups sugar (we use 1 1/3 cups).
1 stick of margarine
3 whole eggs
1/4 cup orange juice (or lemon juice)
grated rind of orange (or lemon)
1 tsp vanilla
1 can Angel Flake Coconut

Melt margarine in sauce pan
over low heat. When barely melted
add sugar and beat. Add whole
                            (beat)
eggs one at a time. And stir in
Add orange juice, vanilla and
rind and coconut.
Pour in unbaked pie shell (we use
                              Ritz)
And cook at 325° till firm
when tested with knife.
30 to 40 minutes.

Key Lime Pie

1 Can Eagle Brand Milk
1 Tablespoon Lime Juice
3 Eggs, Beaten

Directions:

Mix ingredients and fold in the 3 beaten eggs. Pour in Graham Cracker pie shell. Freeze or Refrigerate.

RECIPE FOR: _Key Lime Pie_
1 Can Eagle Brand Milk
1 T Lime juice
Mix and add 3 beaten egg whites
fold in –
Pour in Graham Cracker Shell
Either freeze or Rf

PREPARATION TIME: _____ SERVES: _____
© LAKE   C.R. GIBSON,® NORWALK, CT 06856   Q10-55

Lemon Pie

1 ½ Cup Sugar
½ Cup Cornstarch
1/8 Teaspoon Salt
4 Egg Yolks
1 ¾ Cup Water
½ Cup Lemon Juice
3 Tablespoon Oleo
1 Teaspoon Grated Lemon Rind

Directions:

Combine first 6 ingredients and set aside in sauce pan. Combine egg yolks, water, juice and sugar. Cook on medium heat, stir and boil for 10 minutes. Remove from heat and add oleo and rind.

Lemon Pie   Best
1½ c sugar   ) combine + set aside
½ c cornstarch   ) on sauce pan
1/8 teas Salt
4 egg yolks   ) combine yolks - water + add
1¾ C water   )   juice to sugar
½ C. lemon juice) cook over med heat
3 T oleo   stir + boil 1 min -
1 teas. grated rind   Remove - add oleo +
                                       rind

Lemon Pie by Jackie Thurman

½ Cup Lemon Juice
2 Egg Yolks
1 Can Condensed Milk

Directions:

Mix all ingredients and place in Graham Cracker Crust.

Baking Instructions:

Bake at 350 degrees until Meringue is brown.

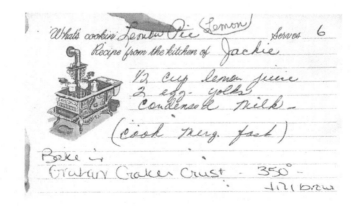

Lemon Pie - Traditional

1 ¼ Cup Sugar
6 Tablespoons Cornstarch
2 Cups Water
1/3 Cup Lemon Juice
3 Eggs Separated
3 Tablespoons Oleo
1 ½ Teaspoon Lemon Extract
2 Teaspoon Vinegar

Directions

Cook in double boiler for 25 minutes. Add the lemon extract, oleo, and vinegar. Stir together and pour in bakes pie shell. Top with Meringue.

Never Fail Meringue

1 Tablespoon Cornstarch
2 Tablespoon Cold Water
½ Cup Boiling Water
3 Egg Whites
6 Tablespoon Sugar
1 Teaspoon Vanilla
Pinch of Salt

Directions:

Mix cornstarch, cold water and boiling water. Cook stirring until clear. Let cool then mix with sugar, vanilla and salt. Then combine both with beaten egg whites.

Never - Fail Meringue

1 T Corn starch) mix   Cook
2 T Cold Water)   stirring
½ cup boiling water add   until
                          clear

3 egg whites   let cool
6 T Sugar   last add to
1 tsp Vanilla   beaten
pinch Salt.   egg white

Pecan Pie

1 Cup Sugar
2 Tablespoon Bourbon
3 Tablespoon Oleo
3 Eggs Beaten Slightly
½ Corn Dark Syrup
1 Cup Pecans

Directions

Combine all ingredients.

Baking Instructions

Bake at 350 degrees until pie is firm.

Recipe: Pecan Pie   Yield: _____
from the kitchen of: _____

1 Cup sugar   2 T bourbon
3 T melted oleo
add 3 eggs - beaten slightly
½ cup Corn syrup (dark)
1 Cup pecans dump in Shell

Pecan Pie by Mildred

1 Cup Sugar
¼ Cup Melted Oleo
½ Cup Dark Corn Syrup
3 Eggs Beaten
1 Cup Pecans
1 Teaspoon Vanilla

Directions

Combine all ingredients.

Baking Instructions

Bake at 400 degrees for 10 minutes then 350 degrees for 30-35 minutes.

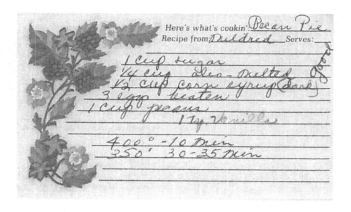

Pecan Pie by Rachel Butler

½ Cup Sugar
1 Teaspoon Flour
2 Whole Eggs Beaten
5 Teaspoons Butter
1 Teaspoon Vanilla
1 Cup Dark Syrup
Pecans

Directions

Mix all ingredients.

Baking Instructions

Bake at 350 degrees until pie is firm.

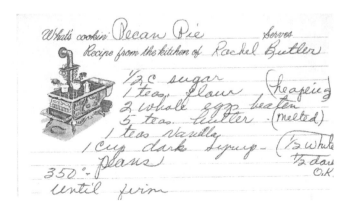

Processor Pie Crusts

2 1/2 Cup Flour
1/2 Teaspoon Salt
6 Tablespoons Butter
6 Tablespoons Crisco
1/2 Cup Cold Water

Directions:

Let set in refrigerator. Makes 2 pie crusts.

RECIPE FOR: Processor Pie Crust

2½ cup flour
½ teas. salt

6 T. butter
6 T. Crisco   = ⅓ cup full

½ cup cold water
let set in ref - Makes 2 pie crust

PREPARATION TIME: _____ SERVES: _____

BAKE   C.R. GIBSON® NORWALK CT 06856   Q10-55

Pumpkin Pie

1 Cup Sugar
1 ½ Teaspoon Cinnamon
½ Teaspoon Cloves
½ Teaspoon Allspice
½ Teaspoon Nutmeg
½ Teaspoon Ginger
½ Teaspoon Salt
2 Whole Eggs, Beaten
1 2/3 Cup Carnation Milk
1 ½ Cup Pumpkin

Directions

Combine all ingredients.

Baking Instructions

Bake at 425 degrees for 15 minutes then bake at 350 degrees at 40 minutes.

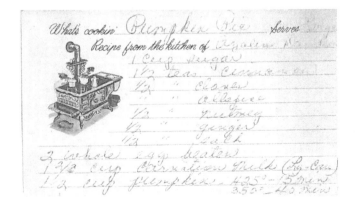

187

Shredded Apple Pies

1 Cup Sugar
1/4 Teaspoon Cinnamon
1 Teaspoon Vanilla
2 Eggs, Beaten
1/2 Stick Oleo, Melted
2 Cups Apple

Directions:

Grate apples. Mix well. put in unbaked shell.

Baking Instructions:

Bake at 400 degrees for 30 minutes.

RECIPE FOR: *Shredded Apple Pie*

1 c. Sugar
1/4 t. cinn.
1 t. vanilla
2 whole eggs (beaten)
1/2 stick oleo melted

Grate 2 c apples — mix well — put in unbaked shell — 400° – 30 min.

PREPARATION TIME: _____ SERVES: _____
© LAKE   C.R. GIBSON,° NORWALK CT 06856   Q10-55

188

Strawberry Pie by Rachel Butler

1 Cup Sugar
1 Cup Water
3 Tablespoon Cornstarch
3 Tablespoon Strawberry Jello
1 Quart Strawberries

Directions

Combine all ingredients and cook.

Here's what's cookin' Strawberry Pie
Recipe from: Rachel Serves:

1 cup Sugar
1 Cup Water
3 T Cornstarch
3 T Strawberry Jello
Cook - add 1 qt berries

Sweet Potato Pie by Sarah White

2 Cup Mashed Sweet Potatoes
¼ Cup Softened Oleo
1 Cup Sugar
½ Teaspoon Salt
1 Teaspoon Cinnamon
1 Teaspoon Nutmeg
¼ Teaspoon Lemon Extract
¼ Teaspoon Almond
2 Teaspoon Vanilla
½ Cup Milk

Directions

Combine all ingredients.

Baking Instructions

Bake at 425 degrees for 10 minutes and then bake at 375 degrees for 1 hour.

Sweet Potato Pie   S. White
2 cup mashed potatoes
¼ cup soft Oleo   425 - 10min
1 cup sugar   375 - 1hr -
½ teas. salt
1 teas. cinnim   unbaked pie
1 " nutmeg   shell
¼ teas. lemon extract
" " Almond
2 teas. Vanilla - 3 eggs - 1½ cup milk

Sweet Potato Pie by Jimmie Ruth Coker

3 tablespoon Flour
1 2/3 Cup Sugar
1 Cup Mashed Sweet Potatoes
2 Eggs
¼ Cup Light Corn Syrup
¼ Teaspoon Nutmeg
Pinch of Salt
½ Cup Oleo
¾ Evaporated Milk

Directions

Mix all ingredients and pour into unbaked pie shell.

Baking Instructions

Bake at 350 degrees for 55-60 minutes.

Sweet Patato Pie   Jimmy Ruth Coker
3 T flour
1 2/3 c sugar
1 Cup mashed S. potatoes
2 eggs
1/4 c light corn syrup
1/4 tsp nutmeg   Mix & pour into
pinch salt   unbaked shell
1/2 c. oleo
3/4 c evap. milk   350° – 55-60 min
          over

Chapter 11: Candy

Chocolate Candy

6 Cubes Chocolate Bark
1 Can Condensed Milk
1/2 Cup Peanut Butter
1/2 Cup Pecans
1 1/2 Teaspoon Vanilla

Directions:

Melt in microwave barks and milk for 5 - 6 minutes. Stir often. Add other
ingredients and stir well. Pour out into butter pan.

Choc. Candy
Choc-Bark - use 6 cubes
1 can condensed Milk (Eagle Brand)
1/2 cup Peanut butter
1/2 cup pecans
1 1/2 tsp. Vanilla
Melt in micr. Barks and milk - Stir often   5-6 min
Add other ing - Stir well -
Pour out in buttered pan

Chocolate Candy by Marie Beckman

2 Cups Sugar
1/3 Cup Cocoa
Small Pet Milk
1 Stick Oleo
1 Teaspoon Vanilla
Nuts

Directions:

Bring sugar, cocoa and milk to boil for 4 minutes. Add oleo, vanilla and nuts. Cool in cold water. Put in 9 x 9 pan.

Choc. Candy   Marie Beckman

2 Cup Sugar)
-1/3 C. Cocoa) boil 4 min.
Sm. Pet milk)

Add 1 stick oleo + 1 teas Vanilla
and Nuts - Cool in Cold Water
Put in 9 by 9 pan -

Chocolate Candy by Sue Foster

3 Cups Sugar
1/2 Cup Cocoa
1 Cup Milk
1 Cup White Syrup
Nuts
1 Teaspoon Vanilla
1/3 Stick Butter

Directions:

Soft ball all ingredients except vanilla and butter. Beat in nuts and vanilla,
then add butter.

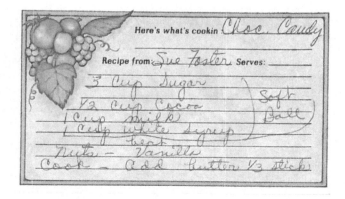

Date Candy by Hazel Baker

3 Cups Sugar
1/2 Cup Milk
1/2 Cup Cream
1/4 Cup Butter
7 1/2 Ounce Pitted Dates
1 Cup Nuts

Directions:

Combine sugar, milk and cream in a sauce pan. Cook without stirring until 236 degrees or soft ball. Add chopped dates, nuts and butter. Let come to a rolling boil. Remove from heat and beat until thick. Spoon onto cloth that has been wrung out in cold water. Form a roll in cloth. When cool slice.

Hazel Baker

Date Candy

3 cups sugar   ½ cup butter
½ cup milk   7½ oz pitted dates
½ cup cream   1 cup nut meats

Combine sugar, milk and cream in a suce pan.
cook without stirring until 236 degrees or
soft ball. Add chopped dates, nuts and
butter. Let come to a rolling ball Remove
from heat and beat until thick. Spoon onto
cloth that has been wrung out in cold water.
form a roll in cloth. When cool slice.

Goo Goo Candy Clusters

by Rachel Butler

12 Ounces Chocolate Chips
12 Ounces Butterscotch Chips
1/4 Cup Peanut Butter
3 Cups Salted Peanuts

Directions:

Mix chips and peanut butter in double boiler. Add peanuts. Drop by small
teaspoon on wax paper.

Goo Goo Candy Clusters Rachel Butler

12 oz. Choc. chips
12 oz. Butterscotch chips
1/4 C. peanut butter
3 C. Salted peanuts
mix chips + peanut butter in double
boiler - Add peanuts - drop by
small teaspoon on wax paper

Microwave Pecan Brittle

1 Cup Sugar
1/2 Cup Corn Syrup
1 Cup Pecan Pieces
1 Teaspoon Oleo
1 Teaspoon Vanilla
1 Cup Baking Soda

Directions:

Combine sugar and syrup in 1 1/2 quart microwave-safe bowl. Microwave
on high for 4 minutes. Stir in pecans. Microwave on high 5 - 7 minutes or
until lightly brown. Stir in oleo and vanilla. Microwave 1 minute. Stir in
soda. Pour onto lightly greased baking sheet. Cool on wire rack. Break
and put in airtight container.

Mints

4 Tablespoon Shortening
1 Box Confectioner's Sugar
12 to 15 Drops of Peppermint
Milk to Moisten to Kneed

From the kitchen of...
Mints

4 T Shortening
1 Box conf. Sugar
12 to 15 drops of peppermint
milk to moisten to kneed

200

Peanut Brittle by Catherine Flatt

3 Cups Sugar
1 Cup Corn Syrup
1 Cup Water
1 Pound Unroasted Peanuts
1 Teaspoon Salt
1 Teaspoon Vanilla
2 Tablespoons Butter
1 Teaspoon Baking Soda

Directions:

Cook sugar, syrup and water until it forms hard ball when tested in cold water. Add the peanuts and continue to cook until slightly caramelized. Remove from heat and add salt, vanilla, butter and soda. Stir until very frothy and pour into a buttered surface. When cooled, slightly break.

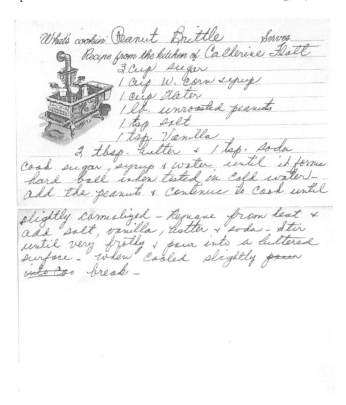

Peanut Butter Balls

2 Sticks Butter, Melted
2 Cups Peanut Butter, Smooth or Crunchy
5 Cups Powdered Sugar
12 Ounces Package Chocolate Chips
1/2 Box of Paraffin Wax

Directions:

Mix butter, peanut butter and sugar together good. Roll in balls.
Chill in refrigerator 30 minutes.

Melt chips in a double boiler. Dip peanut butter balls in chocolate.
Let cool on wax paper.

Peanut Butter Balls
2 sticks Butter (melted)
2 cups peanut butter (smooth or Chunky)
5 cups powdered sugar
mix together good, roll in balls - chill in
refg. 30 min.
            melt in double boiler
12 oz. pack chocolate chips
about ½ bar of paraffin wax
dip ball in chocolate - let cool on wax paper
For variti us coconut - nuts - or raisins

Vanilla Candy by Sue Foster

1 Package Vanilla Bark
2 Tablespoons Peanut Butter
1 Cup Rice Krispies
1 Teaspoon Vanilla
1 Cup Mini Marshmallows
1 Cup Nuts

Directions:

Melt and stir the vanilla bark often. Mix in remaining ingredients and drop
by teaspoon on waxed paper.

6 items
Vanilla Candy   Sue Foster
1 pk. Vanilla Bark) Melt stir
                          often - microw—
Add 2 T peanut butter Stir well
add 1 cup rice crispies
  1 teas vanilla — 1 Cup min marshmellos
  1 cup nuts
mix well then drop by teasspoon
on waxed paper

over

White Fudge

2 1/4 Cup Sugar
1/2 Cup Sour Cream
1/4 Cup Milk
2 Tablespoon Butter
1 Tablespoon Corn Syrup
1/4 Teaspoon Salt
2 Teaspoons Vanilla
1 Cup Chopped Walnuts
1/3 Cup Candied Cherries, Quartered

Directions:

Combine sugar, sour cream, milk, butter, corn syrup, and salt in heavy 2 quart sauce pan. Stir over moderate heat until sugar is dissolved and mixture reaches a boil. Boil 9 - 10 minutes to 238 degrees. Let cool until lukewarm (110 degrees) about one hour. Add vanilla and beat until mixture begins to lose its gloss. Add walnuts and cherries and turn into oiled pan. Let stand until firm before cutting.

Chapter 12: Drinks

Boiled Custard by Sarah

3 Whole Eggs
½ Cup Sugar
1 Quart Milk
1 Teaspoon Vanilla

Directions

Mix eggs and sugar then heat with 1 quart milk on double boiler until it coats spoon and the strain and add vanilla.

From the kitchen of... Sarah
Boiled Custard
3 whole egg) mix
½ cup Sugar)
1 qt milk   Heat
in double boiler
coats spoon – Let
cool + strain
1 tea Vanilla

Egg Custard by Era Allan

1 Cup Sugar
6 Eggs
1 Teaspoon Vanilla
1 Tablespoon Flour
1 Cup Milk
1 Stick Butter
Pinch of Salt

Directions

Sift flour, sugar, salt. Add 5 egg yolks and whole egg. Cook until thick and add butter. Shake nutmeg.

Baking Instructions

Bake at 375 degrees for 30 minutes.

Tea Punch

4-5 Large Tea Bags
3 Cups Sugar
1 Tall Can Pineapple Juice
¼ Cup Lemon Juice
2 Tablespoons Frozen Orange Juice

Tea Punch   1 Gallon

4-5 lg. tea bags
3 cup sugar
1 tall can pineapple juice
1/4 cup lemon juice
2 T frozen orange juice

ABOUT THE AUTHORS

Natalie Henley and Zachery Nace are the grandchild and great grandchild of Daphine Caruthers. They both enjoyed many years of time and love with Daphine. Wanting to continue the traditions their grandmother created with these recipes, the cousins got together to document their grandmother's recipes and life story! The fun from creating the book and the time with their grandmother is priceless.